ISBN 0-9615420-0-4

IF I CAN YOU CAN

DECIPHER GERMANIC RECORDS

by

Edna M. Bentz

Tamara J. Bentz
9150-187 Gramercy Drive
San Diego, CA 92123-4001
tjbentz@prodigy.net

First Printing 1982
Second Printing 1983
Third Printing 1985 (Revised & Corrected)
Fourth Printing 1987 (Additions)
Fifth Printing 1988 (Additions)
Sixth Printing 1989
Seventh Printing 1990 (Additions)
Eighth Printing 1990 (Additions)
Ninth Printing 1991
Tenth Printing 1992 (Color Coded Pages)
Eleventh Printing 1993
Twelfth Printing 1993
Thirteenth Printing 1994
Fourteenth Printing 1995 (Corrections)
Fifteenth Printing 1995 (Additions)
Sixteenth Printing 1996 (Additions)
Seventeenth Printing 1996
Eighteenth Printing 1997 (Additions)
Nineteenth Printing 1997 (Additions)
Twentieth Printing 1998 (Additions)
Twenty-First Printing 1999 (Additions)
Twenty-Second Printing 1999
Twenty-Third Printing 2000
Twenty-Fourth Printing 2001
Twenty-Fifth Printing 2002
Twenty-Sixth Printing 2003
Twenty-Seventh Printing 2005
Twenty-Eighth Printing 2006
Twenty-Ninth Printing 2008

TABLE OF CONTENTS

Dear Friends:

   Just before taking this book to the printer for the 8th printing, I found many new words for illnesses and occupations. Rather than holding up the book for weeks to retype it all, I decided to squeeze them in as best I could so that they would be available to you immediately. Please excuse the irregular spacing.
                                                        – Edna Bentz

F O R E W O R D

When I was old enough to learn to talk, I was fortunate to be able to learn to speak both English and German. After World War I when I started to school, the feelings toward Germans and Germany were not very good. Consequently, my parents decided to speak only English and within a few years I had forgotten how to speak the German language. I had an opportunity in High School to take one year of German. Most of the time was spent on grammar, however I did learn to read and write the old German Script. I loved writing it and would practice by writing notes to my girl friend using English words and old German Script. Incidentally, this is a good way to practice writing the Script and the flow of the letters will become easier. Try copying paragraphs from a book.

Little did I know that almost 50 years later I would be researching Germanic Records trying to find my ancestors and having to read that Script. At first I thought it an impossible job. However, with a little effort to review the letters and practicing, I became more proficient. I still struggle.

I would suggest that you practice writing your surnames. You may want to write them on the back-side of your Alphabet page. Also write the name of the village you are researching and perhaps the names of the villages within a 5-mile radius. This will help you to recognize names, places and dates. Watch the capital K 𝒦 and R 𝑅 as these letters have a similar look. It may save you years of re-searching the wrong village or parish. You may have to build your own alphabet of the record you are researching.

No list can ever be complete. You may find additional occupations or illnesses or phrases, therefore, we have left the back side of the page blank so that you may add your findings. We have compiled these lists from dictionaries, books, records etc. We urge you to have a good German/English, Latin/English or Danish/English dictionary. This manual was written for you to take to the library to give you clues as you read books or microfilm.

I have tried writing the Script using various forms to give you practice. You will have to take into account that handwriting becomes a very individual thing depending on the person doing the writing and where they received their education and the quality of their education. Sometimes you have to count the points as e, i, u, m, and n all look the same. Also sometimes a c if they don't put the hook on.

    Examples: Zimmermann
                 Salzsteuereinnehmer

Watch for the dot over the i that can give you a clue. If there is an umlaut, you will know that it is a vowel. Then there is always the chance that it is an ink blob, speck of dirt on the lens of the microfilm reader or a scratch on the microfilm. You may have to "strick" the word as I call it. Salz|steuer|ein|nehmer and look for the definitions of those individual words.

It would help if you will begin to think in German as you view records. Think "Frau" instead of "wife", "Kinder" instead of "children", "Tochter" instead of "daughter", etc. Soon these terms will become easier to decipher. Write the German term in your notes so that you do not interrupt your thinking. You can translate to English later when you enter the data on your family sheets. As you become better at deciphering this Script, you may want to go back over film that you viewed before. You may be surprised at what you have missed.

My thanks to my friends in the German Research Association of San Diego who have encouraged me to put this book together, and to my family who go to sleep every night with the clack of the type-writer. Also my thanks to my daughter Tamara who helped put together the time-line. We continue to learn and realize how little we know when we step out into places where angels fear to tread.

As former Editor of The German Connection, I was continually looking for helps for our members so that they could become more proficient in deciphering Germanic records. It is my hope that this book will be of help to you.

I want to encourage you to continue to work because
IF I CAN YOU CAN DECIPHER GERMANIC RECORDS.

ALPHABET

The first form of each letter given is the more common form used. however, the other forms may be used in various parts of the Germanic speaking countries. You may want to build your own alphabet using the forms found on a particular record.

ALPHABET (Continued)

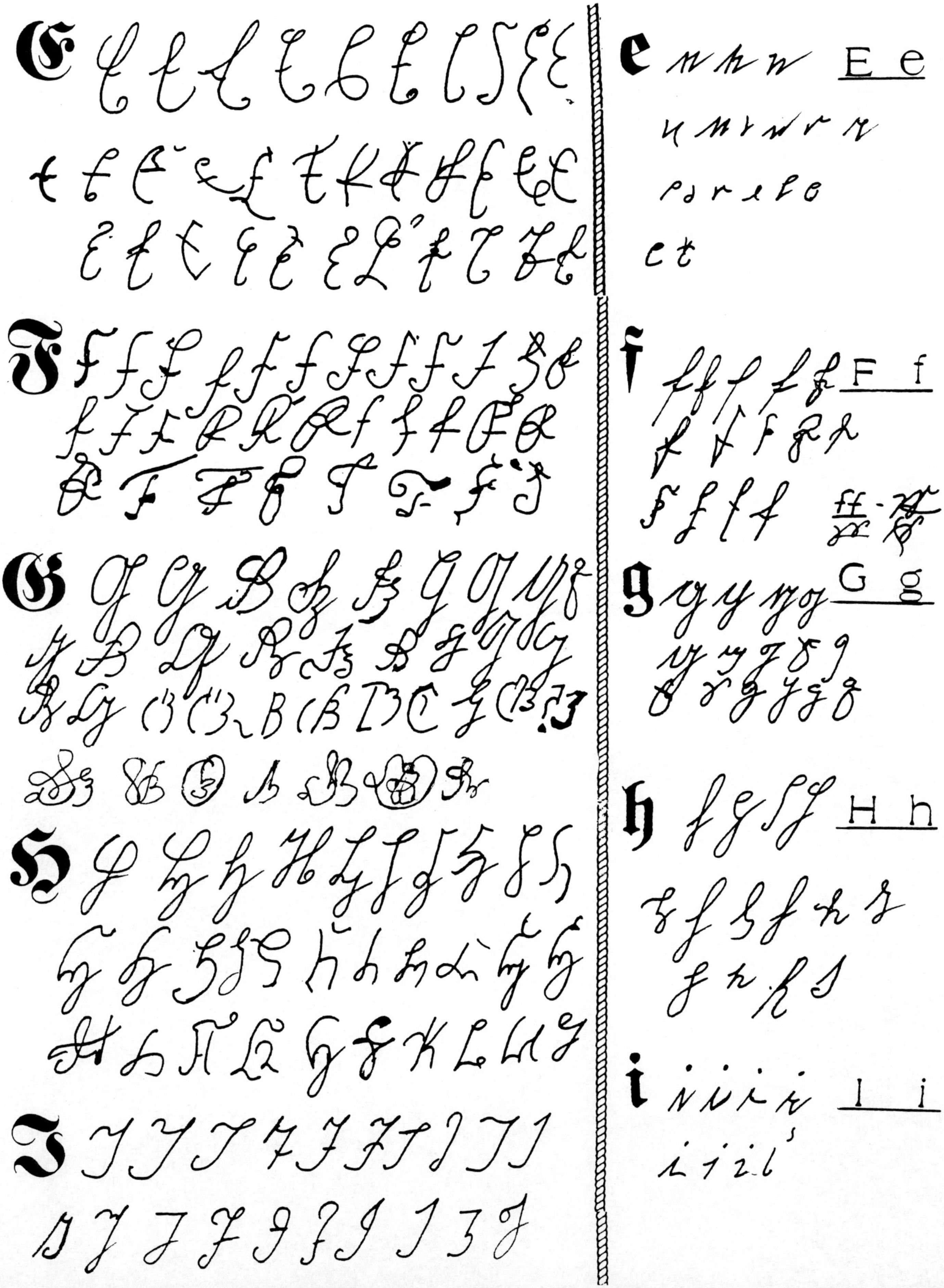

ALPHABET (Continued)

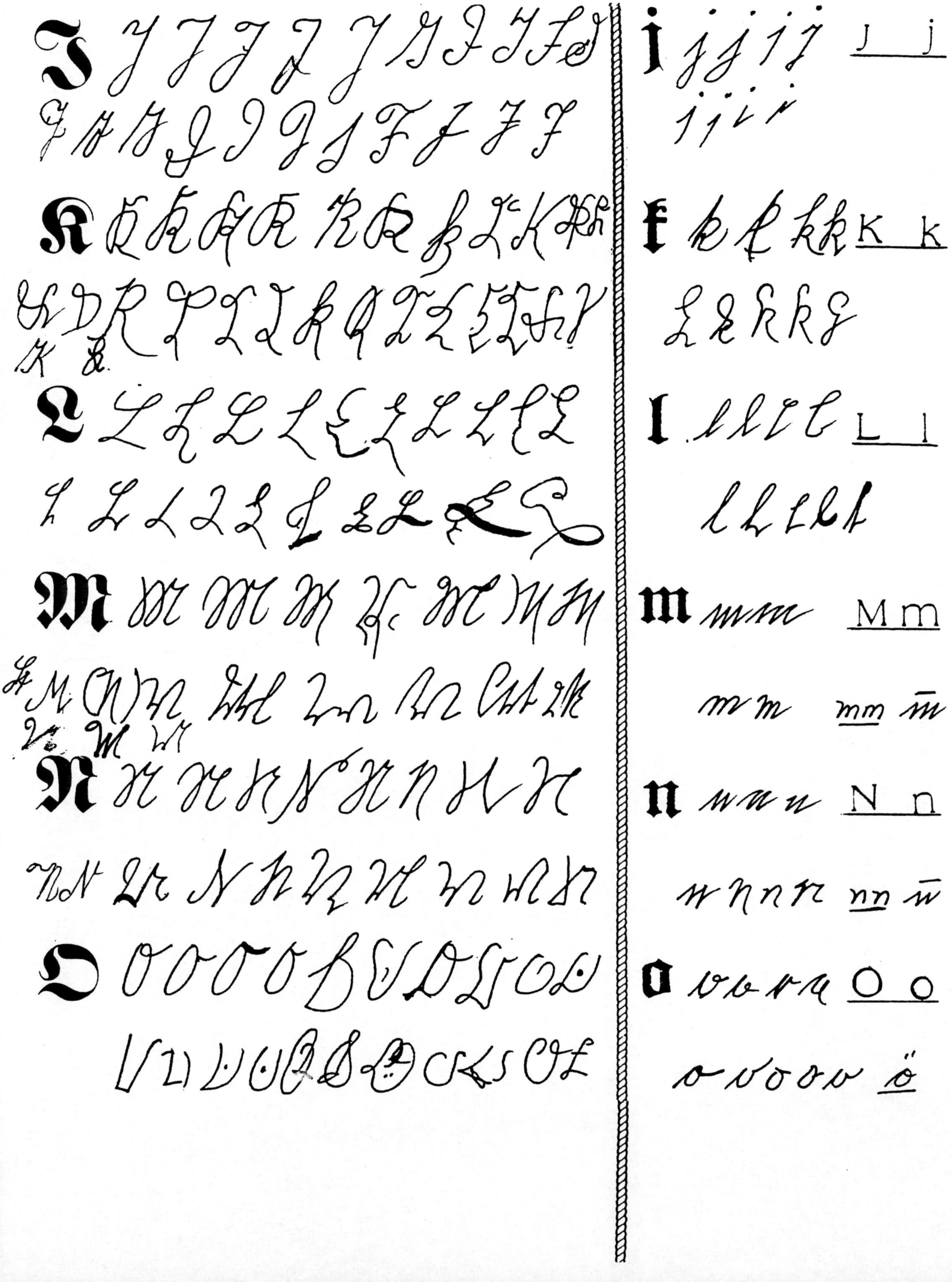

ALPHABET (Continued)

P p
Q q
R r
S s
(always at the end of words or syllables)
St
st
Sch
sch
(at the end of a word)
SS
(always following vowels)
T t
Tz

ALPHABET (Continued)

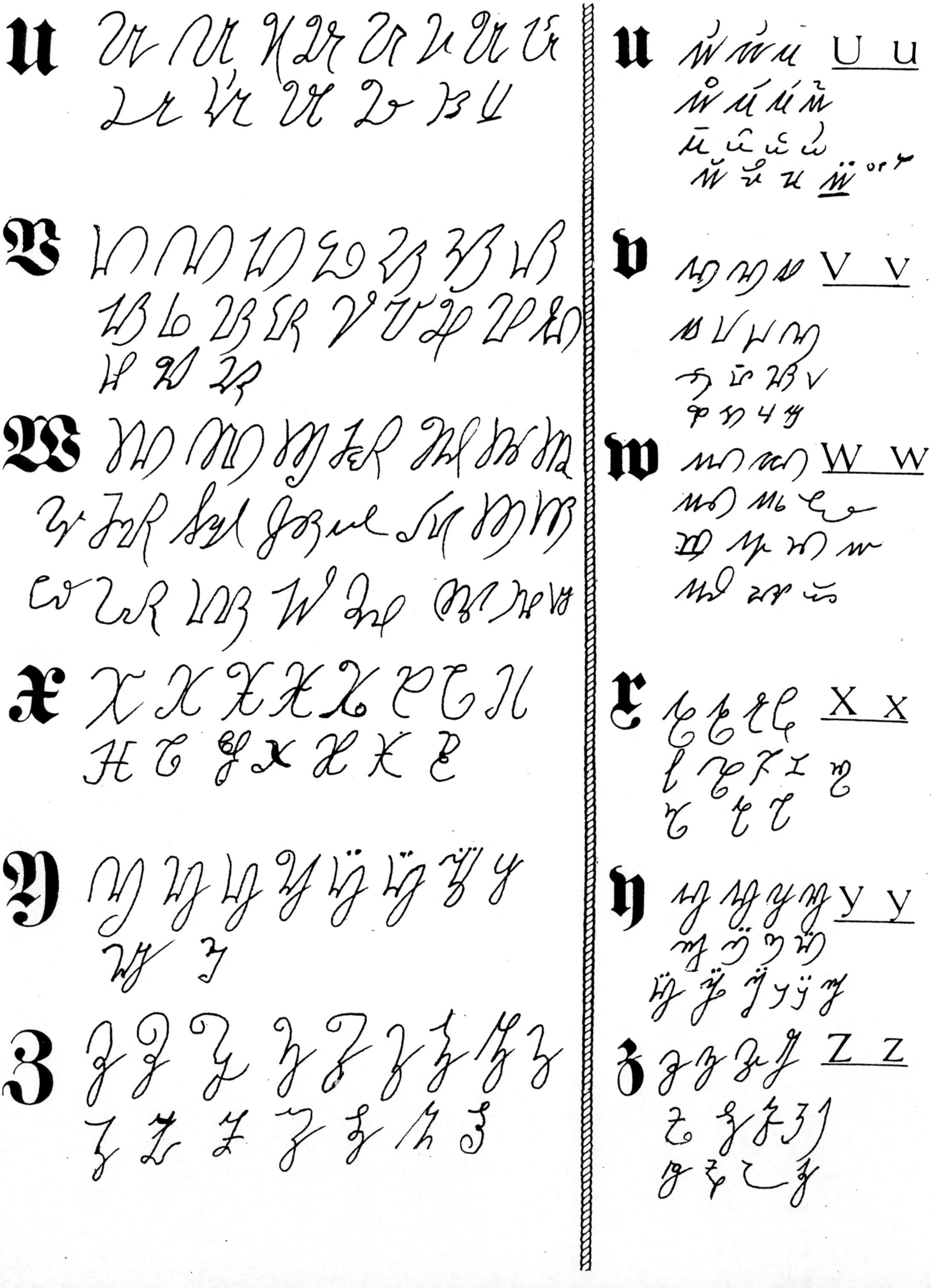

ANOTHER GOTHIC ALPHABET

Following is another Gothic Alphabet including old forms which was used in DANISH genealogical records. Those of you who are researching in Schleswig-Holstein area that was at one time under the Danish rule, may find this variation helpful. I have found that squiggly G and that 5th and 6th C.

CAPITAL LETTERS | SMALL LETTERS

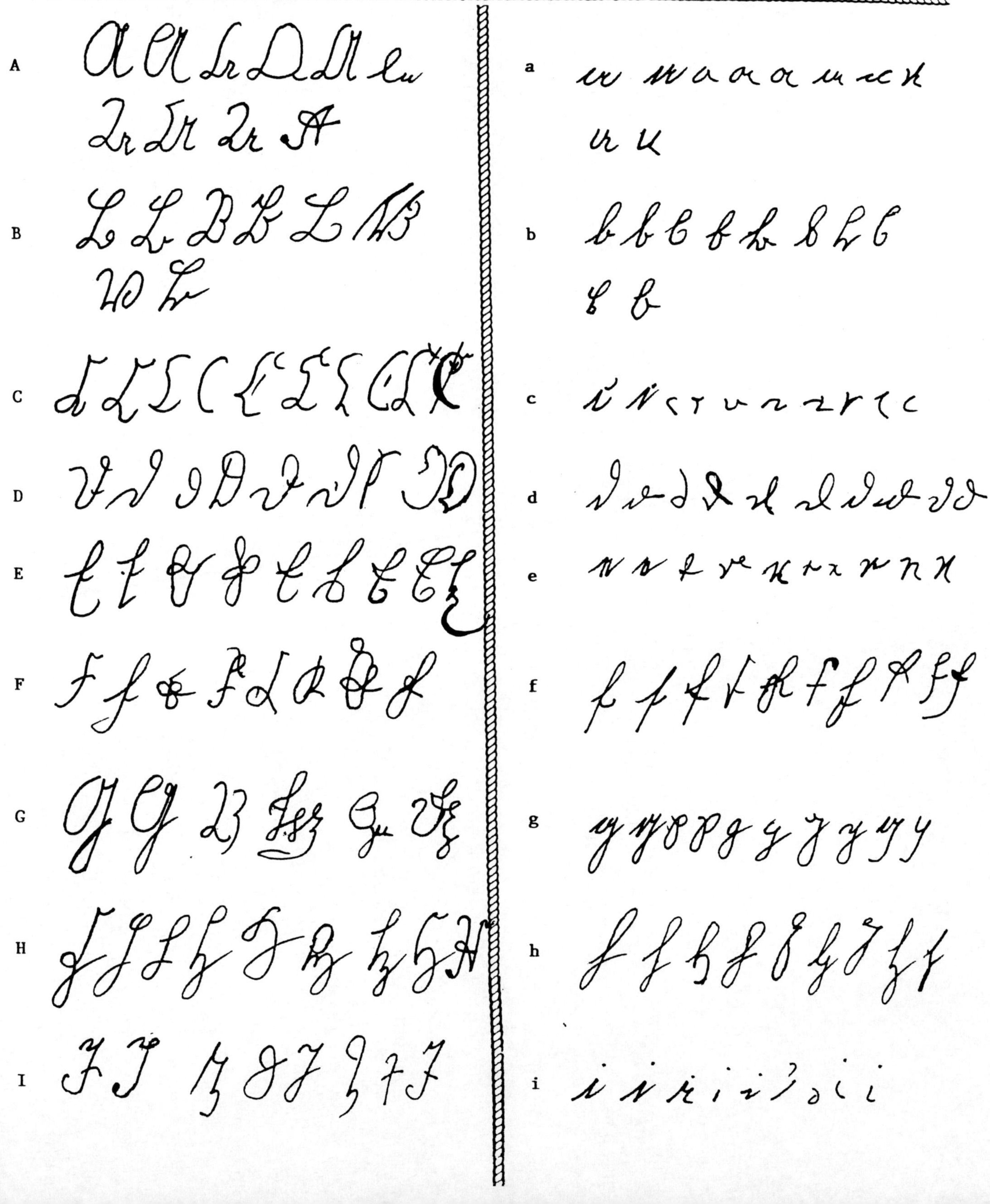

J	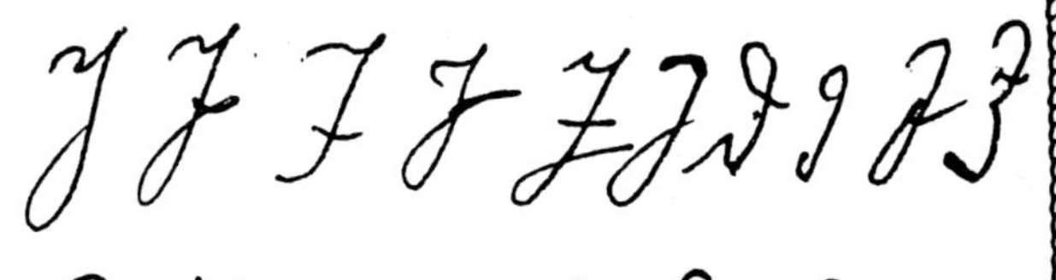	j	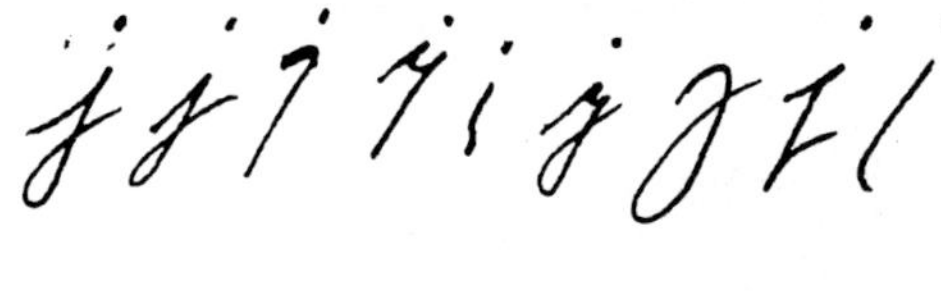
K	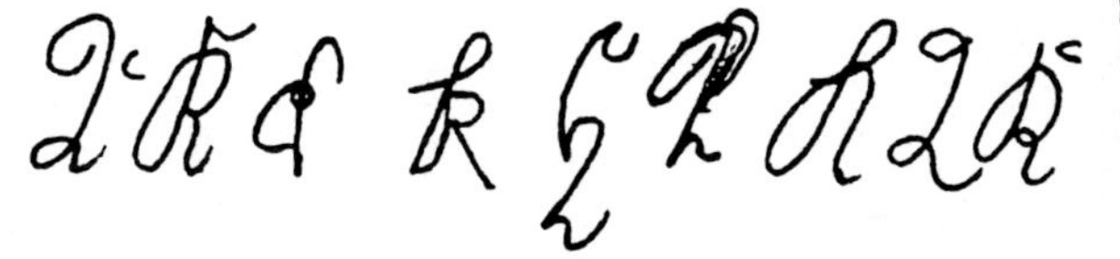	k	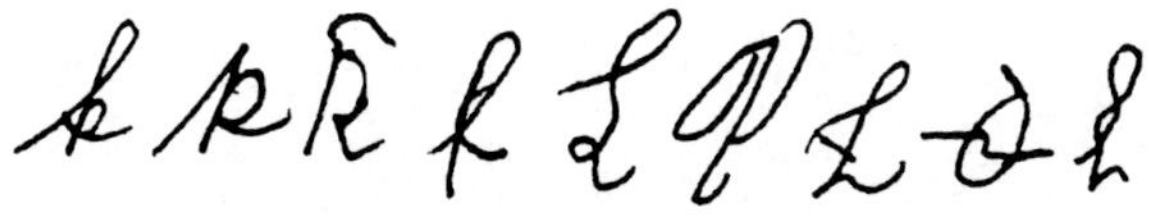
L	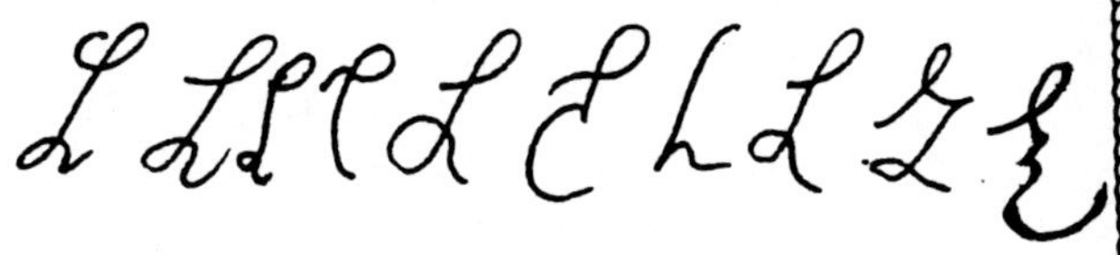	l	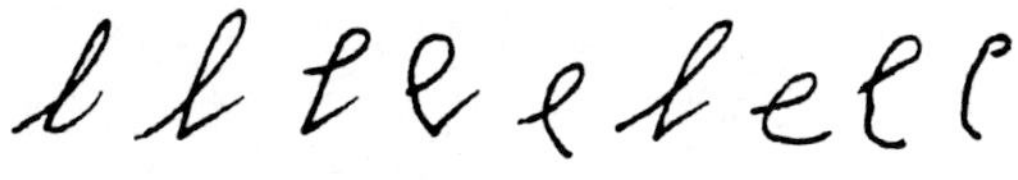
M	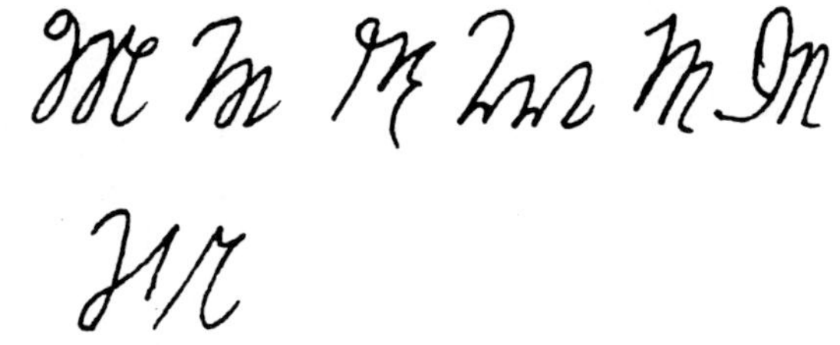	m	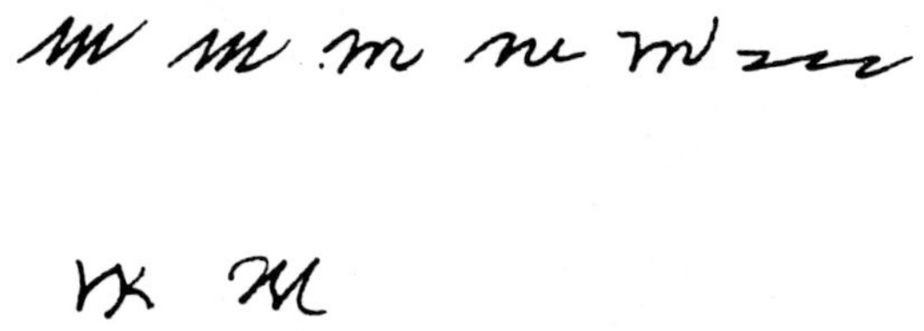
N	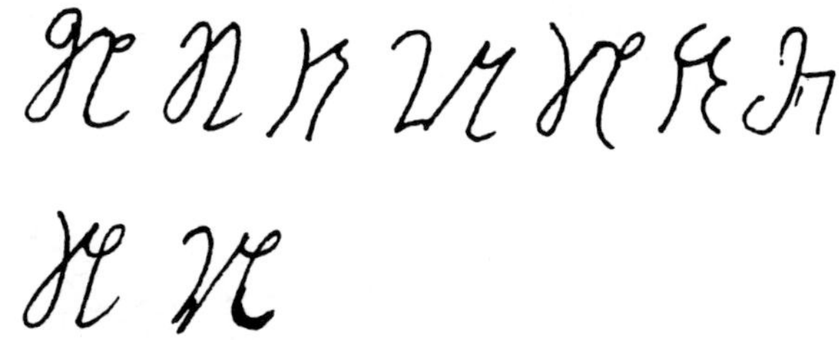	n	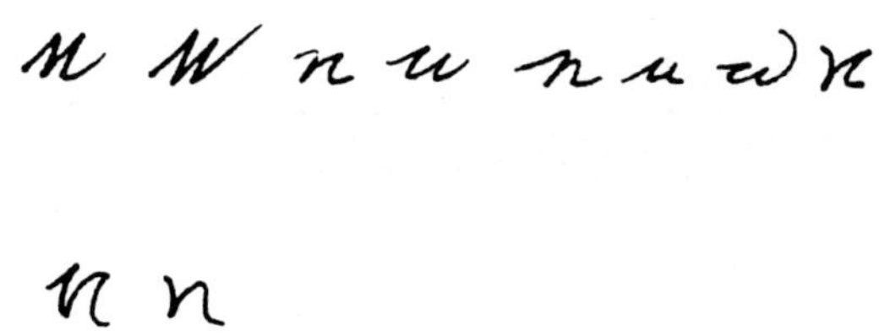
O	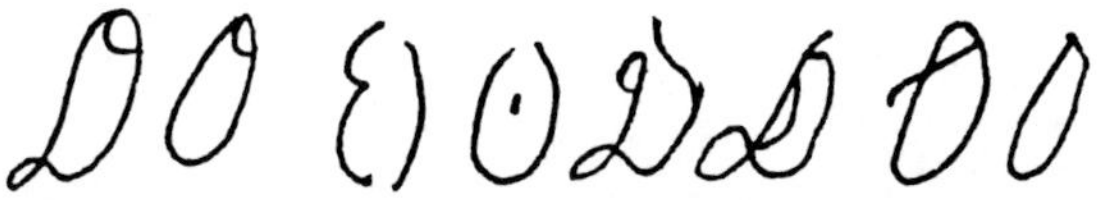	o	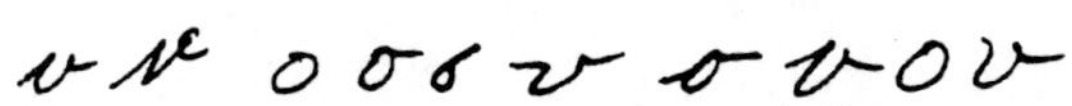
P	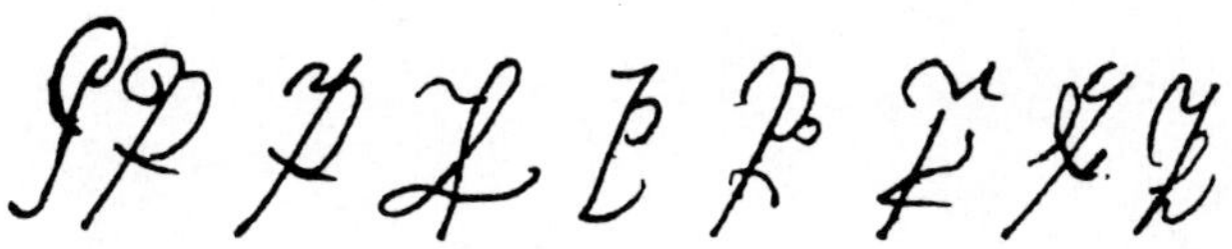	p	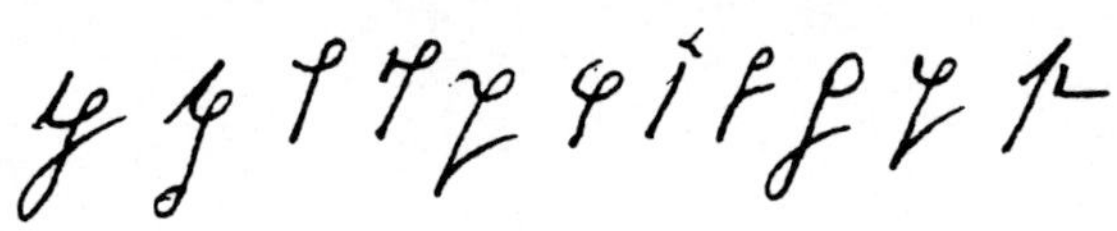
Q	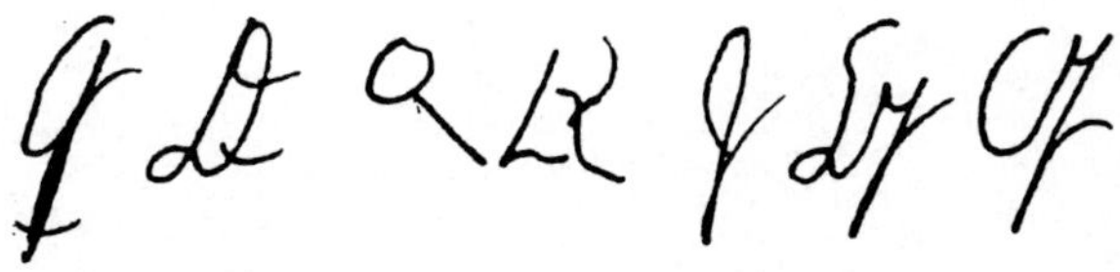	q	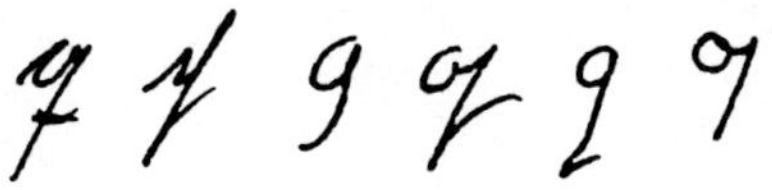
R	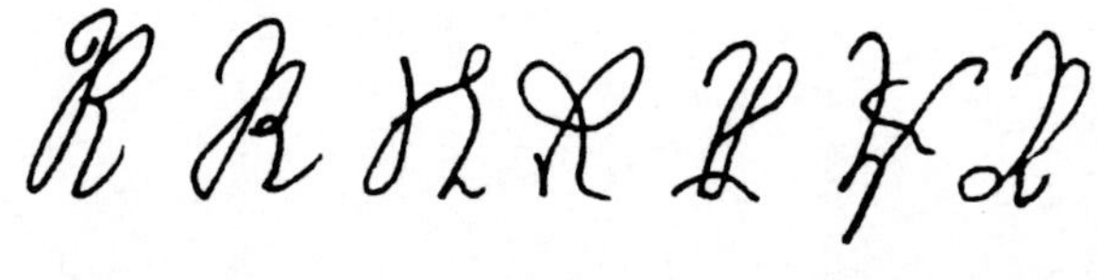	r	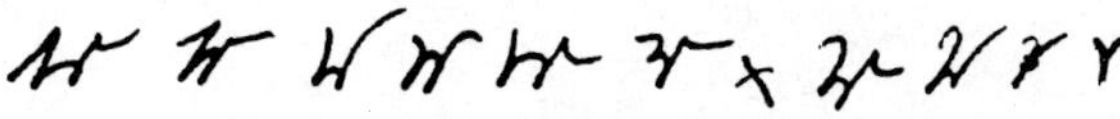
S	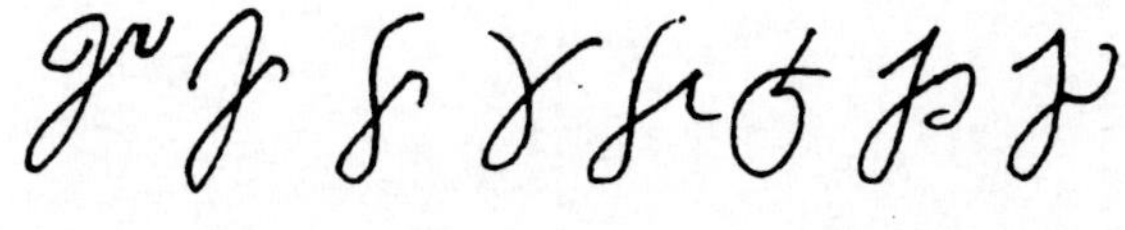	s	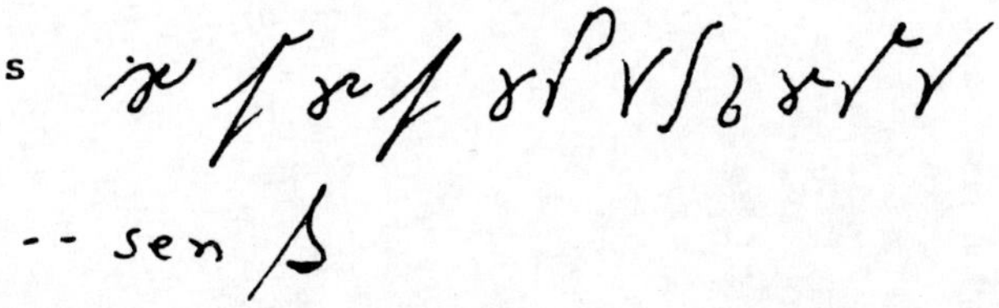

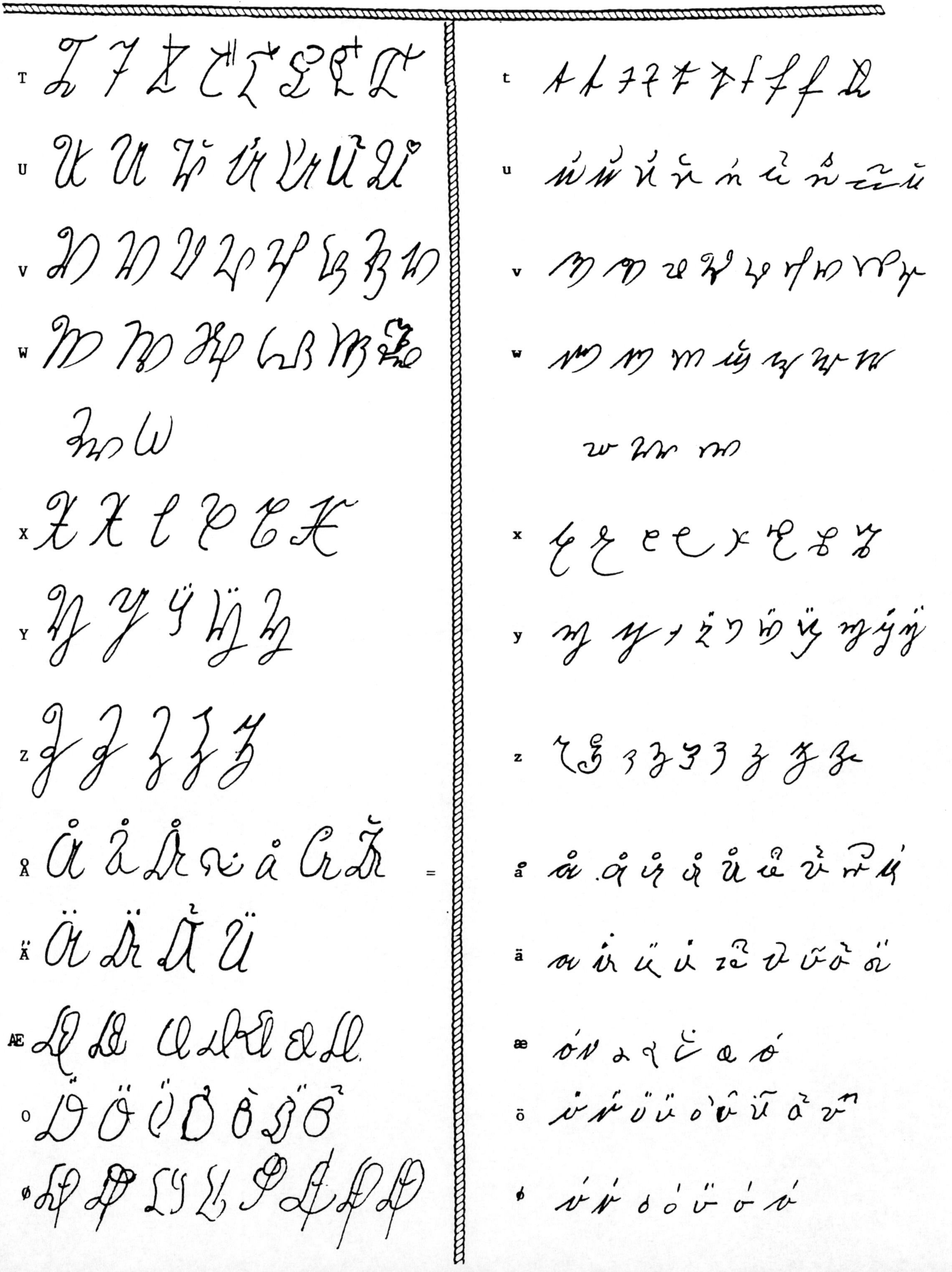
T
U
V
W
X
Y
Z
Å
Ä
Æ
O
Ø
=
t
u
v
w
x
y
z
å
ä
æ
ö
ø

a, o, and u are sometimes found with umlauts.

Example: ̋a ä   ̋o ö   ̋u ü   You may find a ȳ ÿ with an umlaut

EXAMPLES OF SURNAMES USING THE UMLAUT

Rödlingschöfer *(handwritten)* could be Roedlingschoefer *(handwritten)*

Müller *(handwritten)* could be Mueller *(handwritten)*

Schäfer *(handwritten)* could be Schaefer *(handwritten)*

Rückert *(handwritten)* could be Rueckert *(handwritten)*

Göß *(handwritten)* could be Goeß *(handwritten)*

Göhs *(handwritten)* could be Goehs *(handwritten)*

Götz *(handwritten)* could be Goetz *(handwritten)*

Käs *(handwritten)* or Käß *(handwritten)* could be Kaes *(handwritten)* Kaeß *(handwritten)*

GENERAL INFORMATION

Umlauts are used to change the sounds of the vowels. A a, O o, U u, but not E e and I i

c is used before the letters h or k -example: ch *(handwritten)*   or ck *(handwritten)*

Sometimes in the sch the c is hard to see - example: *(handwritten)*

ALL German words, when used as nouns are <u>capitalized</u>.
   Some preachers also capitalize adjectives

The pronoun, ich *(handwritten)* (I), is not capitalized except at the beginning of a sentence.

DO NOT EXPECT ALL GRAMMATICAL RULES TO ALWAYS BE FOLLOWED. One will often find:
   1. words misspelled   4. dialect words and phrases
   2. umlauts missing   5. improper word order
   3. lack of punctuation   6. nouns not capitalized
                                  7. hyphen missing

SURNAMES: Remember the name will be spelled the way the preacher spelled the name.
            It is possible-new preacher - new spelling
            If the family moved it may be spelled a different way in another village.

Example: my grandfather - the name Meyer in Ottenhofen, Mittelfranken, Bavaria
          my great-grandfather - the name Meier in Westheim, Mittelfranken, Bavaria
          my 2nd great-grandfather- the name Mayer in Marktbergel, Mittelfranken, Bavaria
          my 3rd great-grandfather- the name Meÿer in Obernzenn, Mittelfranken, Bavaria

"in" suffix was sometimes added to the surnames of <u>females</u>. Ex: Goess - Goessin
"lein" suffix was sometimes added to surnames of same family. Ex: Merk - Merklein

INTERCHANGEABLE LETTERS

D - T - Th	Ex:	Durauf - Thurauf	P - B	Ex:	Plank - Blank
Ch - GR	Ex:	Christof - Gristof	tt - f	Ex:	Ittner - Iffner
C - K	Ex:	Conrad - Konrad	I - Y - J	Ex:	Jetter - Yetter
F - V	Ex:	Fischer - Vischer	t - th	Ex:	Walter - Walther
Pf - F	Ex:	Pfaler - Fehler			

RELATIONSHIPS

Most of the time you will be working from the German Script-to the German word-to the English word.   I have tried to arrange this list in alphabetical order starting with the script.

SCRIPT	GERMAN	ENGLISH
	angenommenes Kind	adopted child
	Adoptiert	adopted
	Base	female cousin or kinswoman or aunt
	Blutsverwandschaft	blood relationship
	Bruder	brother
	Ehefrau	wife, housewife
	Ehemann	husband
	Eltern	parents
	Enkel	grandson
	Enkelkind	grandchild
	Enkelin	granddaughter
	Erbe	heir
	Gatte	husband
	Findling	foundling
	Gattin	wife
	Gemahl (in)	spouse, husband, wife
	Geschwisterkind	sister's child or brother's child
	Geschwister	siblings, brothers or sisters
	Gevatter	godfather
	Gevatterin	godmother
	Großeltern	grandparents
	Großmutter	grandmother
	Großvater	grandfather
	Kinder	children
	Kusine	cousin
	liebliche Base (cherished)	first female cousin
	lieblicher Vetter (cherished)	first male cousin
	Mutter	mother
	Nebenfrau	concubine

RELATIONSHIPS (Continued)

SCRIPT	GERMAN	ENGLISH
	Neffe	nephew
	Nichte	niece
	Nicht bekannt	not known
	Onkel, Oheim	uncle
	Patenkind	godchild
	Plegesohn (tochter)	Foster son or daughter
	Schwager	brother-in-law
	Schwägerin	sister-in-law
	Schwester	sister
	Schwiegermutter	mother-in-law
	Schwiegervater	father-in-law
	Schwippschwager	Ex: she married brother of sister's husband
	Sohn	son
	Söhner	Daughter-in-law
	Stiefkind	Step-child
	Stiefmutter	step-mother
	Stiefvater	step-father
	Tante	aunt
	Taufpate	godfather
	Taufpatin	godmother
	Tochter	daughter
	Unbekannte	unknown
	Urenkelkind	great-grandchild
	Urgroßmutter	great-grandmother
	Urgroßvater	great-grandfather
	Vater	father
	Vetter	male cousin or kinsman or uncle
	Vorkind	step-children from previous marriage

I have tried to use various forms of the letters to give you practice in reading.
Different areas of the country may have used different forms.

GENEALOGICAL TERMINOLOGY AND SYMBOLS

SCRIPT	GERMAN	ENGLISH	SYMBOLS
	Ahnen	ancestor	
	Ahnentafel	pedigree chart	
	andere Ehe	other marriage	
	auswandern	to emigrate	
	Begräbnis	burial or funeral	▭ or ⚰
	Begräbnisstätte	cemetery	
	Beruf	occupation	
	Braut Kind	child born before the marriage	
	Ehe	marriage	oo or oo or ⊗
	Ehebrecher	adulterer	
	ehelich	legitimate	
	Ehescheidung	divorce	o|o or o|o or o/o
	evangelisch	Protestant	
	Familie	family	
	Familiename	family name	
	freie Verbindung	illegitimate union (common law)	O—O or o—o
	Friedhof	cemetary	
	Geburt (geb.)	birth	* or * or ✳
	Gemeinde (Gem.)	community, parish	
	genannt	known as	
	geschieden	divorced	o|o or o/o or o|o
	gestorben (gest.)	died	✝ or +
	getraut	wed	OO or oo or ∞
	Halbbruder	half-brother	
	Halbschwester	half-sister	
	Hebamme	midwife	
	Hebräer	Hebrew	
	Heirat or Heirath (old form)	marriage, copulation	oo or oo or ⊗
	Hochzeit, Hillcheit, Hileich,	wedding ceremony	

SCRIPT	GERMAN	ENGLISH	SYMBOLS
	Hurenkind	illegitimate child of a woman who has had other illegitimate children by other partners	
	Katholiker	Catholic	
	katholisch	Catholic	
	kinderlos	childless	
	Kirchhof	burying ground	♈
	konfirmiert (confirmiert)	confirmed	
	ledig	single	
	Leichenverbrennung	cremation	⚱ or 🪔
	lutherisch	Lutheran	
	Mädchenname	maiden name	
	mennonitisch	Mennonite	
	noch lebende	still living	
	protestantisch	Protestant	
	reformiert	Reformed	
	Schein	certificate	
	Selbstmord	suicide	
	sterben	death	† or + or ⴕ
	Taufe	baptism	∿ or ⌣ or A
	Tod (t)	death	† or + or ⴕ
		died of wounds (battle)	†✗
		died in battle	✗ ✗
	todtgeboren	stillborn	ⴕ or †* or +*
	unbekannt	unknown	
	unehelich	illegitimate	(✳) or (*) or 0-0 or -/
	verheiratet (verheirathet old form)	married	∞ or oo / X or X
	verlobt	engaged	o or o
	Vorfahr	ancestor	
	Vornamen	first name	

GENEALOGICAL TERMINOLOGY AND SYMBOLS (Continued)

SCRIPT	GERMAN	ENGLISH	SYMBOLS
(script)	Waise	orphan	
(script)	Wehmutter	midwife	
(script)	Witwe	widow	
(script)	Witwer	widower	
(script)	Wohnort	place of residence	
(script)	Zeuge	Witness	
(script)	Zwilling	twin	
		line extinct	††
		* confiscated property	*(symbol)*
		* l before a date means they were living on this date	*(symbol)* l
		* S before a date means they died on that date	*(symbol)*
	* used by German Genealogists		

COMMON ABBREVIATIONS

Ca.	= circa (about)
nat.	= natus, nata (born)
ren.	= renatus, renata (baptized)
spur.	= spurius, spuria (illegitimate)
eod.	= eodem (the smae)
ux.	= uxor (wife)
vid.	= viduus, vidua (widower, widow)
N.N.	= nomen nescio (name not known)
S.d.	= Sohn des, Sohn der (son of)
S.v.	= Sohn von (son of)
T.d.	= Tochter des, Tochter der (daughter of)
u.d.	= und des, und der (and of)
ehel.	= ehelich (legitimate)
mannl.	= männlich (masculine)
weibl.	= weiblich (feminine)

1782 *(script)* 1 Mai = year was right but the day and month was "told to them"

Pfr.	= Pfarrer (minister)
weil.	= weiland (deceased)
b.v.	= beide von (both from
Jfr.	= Jungfrau (maiden, virgin)
A.D.H.	= aus dem Hause (out of the house)
d.d.	= de dato (on this date)

verh.	= verheiratet (married)
geb.	= geboren (born) maiden name
get.	= getauft (baptized, christened)
gest.	= gestorben (died)
verl.	= verlobt (engaged)
getr.	= getraut (married)
u.	= und (and)
v.	= von (from)
e.r.	= errore reservata = vorbehaltlich Irrtum (error reserved
e. et. O. R.	= errore et omissione reservata
st.n	= stilo novo (new style of dating a document)
samt.	= together with
evang.	= evangelisch
ejusd.	= ejusdem (in the same month or year
led.	= ledig (single)
ao.	= Anno (year
Magd.	= servant girl, maid
Wwe	= Witwe (widow)
Wwer	= Witwer (widower)

The church year begins with the season of Advent. There are fixed dates and movable dates.

THE SEASON OF ADVENT - Four Weeks		Advent
The First Sunday in Advent (the Sunday nearest St. Andrew's Day		
St. Andrew, Apostle	November 30	
St. Thomas, Apostle	December 21	
CHRISTMAS DAY, The Nativity of Our Lord	December 25	Weihnacht
St. Stephen, Martyr	December 26	
St. John, Apostle, Evangelist	December 27	
The Holy Innocents	December 28	
The Circumcision of Our Lord	January 1	Fest der Beschneidung Christi
THE SEASON OF EPIPHANY - One to Six Sundays		Epiphanias or Erscheinung Christi
The Epiphany of Our Lord	January 6	
Septuagesima Sunday (9 weeks before Easter)		
Sexagesima Sunday (8 weeks before Easter)		
Quinquagesima Sunday (7 weeks before Easter)		
The Conversion of St. Paul	January 25	
The Presentation of Our Lord	February 2	Fest der Reinigung Mariä
St. Matthias, Apostle	February 24	

THE SEASON OF LENT - Forty Days

Ash Wednesday, The First Day of Lent		Aschermittwoch Fastenzeit
The Sundays in Lent	I Invocavit (6 wks.bfr.Easter)	
	II Reminiscere (5 wks.bfr.Easter)	
	III Oculi (4 wks.bfr.Easter)	
	IV Laetare (3 wks,bfr.Easter)	
	V Judica, Passion Sunday (2 wks.bfr.Easter)	Passionssonntag
	VI Palmarum, Palm Sunday (1 wk.bfr.Easter)	Palmsonntag
The Days in Holy Week	Monday	
	Tuesday	
	Wednesday	
	Maundy Thursday	Danksagung or Gründonnerstag
	Good Friday	Sterben Jesu Christi or Karfreitag
	Saturday, Easter Eve	

THE EASTER (or Paschal) SEASON		Osterzeit
Easter Day, The Resurrection of Our Lord		or Auferstehung Jesu Christi
The Annunciation	March 25	Fest der Verkündigung Maria
The Sundays after Easter	I Quasi Modo Geniti (1 wk.aft. Easter)	
	II Misericordia	
	III Jubilate	
	IV Cantate	
	V Rogate	
The Ascension of Our Lord	Thursday	Himmelfahrt Christi
The Sunday after the Ascension (VI) Exaudi		
St. Mark, Evangelist	April 25	
St. Philip and St. James, Apostles	May 1	
THE DAY OF PENTECOST, Witsunday (7 wks.aft.Easter)		Pfingst-Fest or Pfingsten

THE TRINITY SEASON(Season after Pentecost 22-27 weeks)		Trinitatis
Trinity Sunday		
The Nativity of St. John the Baptist	June 24	Fest Johannis des Täufers
St. Peter and St. Paul, Apostles	June 29	
The Visitation	July 2	Fest der Heimsuchung Mariä
St. James the Elder, Apostle	July 25	
The Transfiguration of Our Lord	August 6	Ungestaltung or Verklärung Christi
Assumption of Mary (Catholic church only)	August 15	
St. Bartholomew, Apostle	August 24	
St. Matthew, Apostle, Evangelist	September 21	
St. Michael and All Angels	September 29	Michaelis-Fest
St. Luke, Evangelist	October 18	
St. Simon and St. Jude, Apostles	October 28	
Reformation Day (Lutheran and Protestant churches)	October 31	Reformation-Fest
All Saints' Day	November 1	Allerheiligen
All Souls' Day (Nov. 3 if Nov. 2 is Sunday)	November 2	Allerseelen

MONTHS OF THE YEAR

SCRIPT	GERMAN	OLD FORM	ENGLISH
Jänner	Januar	Jänner, Hartung, Eismonat	January
Februar	Februar	Feber, Hornung, Regenmonat	February
März	März	Lenzing, Lenzmond, Windmonat	March
April	April	Ostermonat, Ostermond, Wandelmonat	April
Mai	Mai	Weidemonat, Wonnemond, Blütenmonat	May
Juni	Juni	Brachet, Brachmonat, Wiesemonat	June
Juli	Juli	Heuert, Heumonat	July
August	August	Ernting, Erntemonat, Hitzmonat	August
September	September	Fruchmonat, Scheiding, 7ber, 7bris	September
October	October	Weinmonat, Gilbhard, 8ber, 8bris	October
November	November	Reifmonat, Nebelmonat, 9ber, 9bris	November
Dezember	Dezember	Julmonat, Christmonat 10ber, 10bris	December

DAYS OF THE WEEK

SCRIPT	GERMAN	ENGLISH	SYMBOLS
Sontag	Sontag	Sunday	☉ or ☉
Montag	Montag	Monday	☽ or ☾ or ☽
Dienstag	Dienstag	Tuesday	♂
Mittwoch	Mittwoch	Wednesday	☿
Donnerstag	Donnerstag	Thursday	♃
Freitag	Freitag	Friday	♀
Samstag	Samstag or	Saturday	♄ or ♄
Sonnabend	Sonnabend or		
Satertag	Satertag		

	GERMAN	ENGLISH	
den	den	on the	
der	der – m	the	
die	die – f	the	
das	das – n	the	

For those of you who are working in Roman Catholic Parish records, I wanted to give you a list of Latin terms. I am including the terminology in the old German script. For those working in the Schleswig-Holstein area during the Danish rule,* I have included the Danish word. This list is alphabetical according to the Latin. I have gathered this material using an English-Latin, English-New Norwegian to old Danish dictionaries. In some cases I could not find a single word, therefore, I have included several words that may give you a clue.

GERMANIC LATIN AND DANISH TERMINOLOGY

LATIN	ENGLISH	GERMAN SCRIPT	DANISH
abortivus, abortio	abortion, stillborn	*(script)*	abort, dødfødt
absterus	baptized	*(script)*	døpt, døbt, daab
accensus	community or parish	*(script)*	samfund, sogn
aqua renatus spirituali	water	*(script)*	vatn
acqua	baptized home christening	*(script)*	døpt, døbt, daab hjemmedøbt
ava avia	grandmother	*(script)*	bestemoder bestemor
avunculus	maternal uncle or great uncle	*(script)*	moderlig onkel
avus	grandfather	*(script)*	bestefader bestefar
avi, avorum	grandparents	*(script)*	besteforeldre
bellum	war	*(script)*	krig
cadaver	dead body	*(script)*	død
caelebs, caelibis	bachelor unmarried man	*(script)*	ungkarl, unkar
nuptias celebrare	to marry	*(script)*	gifte
cimiterium, coemeterium	cemetery	*(script)*	kirkegaard, kirkegård
civilis	civil	*(script)*	sivil
civis, burgensis	citizen	*(script)*	borger, sivilist
civitas	city	*(script)*	stad

* 1448 King Christian I. Denmark inherits Schleswig-Holstein   1773 Holstein ceded to Denmark 1864-1920 German rule -plus area up to Ribe 1920-North Schleswig given back to Denmark

GERMANIC LATIN AND DANISH TERMINOLOGY (Continued)

LATIN	ENGLISH	GERMAN SCRIPT	DANISH
coitus	sexual union		kjønns forening
coelebs	single		ugift
coemeterium	cemetary		kirkegård
commater	godmother		gudmor, gudmoder
compater	godfather		gudfar, gudfäder
conceptus	conceived		unnfange (conceive)
confirmatio	confirmed		Kirke/ståpåket (to be confirmed)
conceptus/a iniquo coitu	conceived in/by a sinful sexual union		synde (sinful)
conjugatus	married, joined		gift, vie
conjugata	wife		hustru, kone, frue
conjugatus	husband		ektemann,
coniuges	spouses		ektefelle, ektemake
coniunx, coniugis	spouse, married person		ektemake, ektefelle
decessit	he/she died		(he)han, den dø (she)hun, den dø
decessus	death, decease		død
defunctus	dead, deceased		død, dødsfall
didymi	twin		trilling
dismissoriales	dismissory letters granting leave to depart one parish or dioceses in order to enter another		send ebort
divortatus	divorce		skilsmisse
domicilium	house, domicile		hus, bopel, hjemsted
domoemigrans	to emigrate		esmigrere
domus	house, home		hus, hjem, heim
ducatus	duchy		hertugdømme
ecclesia	church		kirke

LATIN	ENGLISH	GERMAN SCRIPT	DANISH
elutus	baptized (lit.washed off)		døpe
familia	family		familie
femina foemina	woman, wife		hun
filia	daughter		datter, dotter
filiola	little daughter		liten datter
filiolus	little son		liten sønn
filius	son		sønn
frater	brother		bror, broder
geminus	twin		tvilling
geminae arum (f/pl)	twin daughters		tvilling datter
gemini orum (m/pl)	twin sons or son & daughter		tvilling sønn tvilling sønn og datter
gener	son-in-law		svigersønn
glos	sister-in-law		svigerinne
numatus	buried		begravet
illegitimus	illegitimate		uekte
imperitus	unskilled untrained		uøvd (untrained) uoppltst (uned.)
incola	inhabitant, resident		beboer, bebo innbygger
infans (m)	infant, child		litt barn, barn
infantis (f)	infant, child		litt barn, barn
intronixo	to wed, marry		gifte, ekte
Junior	junior, younger		yngre, yngst

LATIN	ENGLISH	GERMAN SCRIPT	DANISH
juvenis	young man		ung menneske
lautus	baptized, washed		døbt
liberus	childless		barn mindre ?
vevir	brother-in-law		svigerbroder
ligatus	bound, joined; married		bestemt, copulerat, forbinde, gift
legitimus	legitimate		ektefødd, aegte
majorennis	of legal age		? alder
maritatio	marriage		aekterviede, aegteviede (married)
marita (f)	spouse, wife, married woman		ecktefelle, hustru, kone, frue
martio	to wed, marry		eckte (marry)
maritus	spouse, husband, married man		ecktefelle, ectemann, aegtemand
masculinus	male		mann, mand, mannlig
mater	mother		mor, moder
matrimonium	marriage		aekterviede, aegter-viede (married)
matrina	godmother		gudmor, gudmoder
matrinia	step-mother		- - -
mixtus	mixed(i.e,marriage: one a Catholic, one not)		ekteskap mellom Protesant og Katolikk
mortus	dead, died		død
naturalis	illegitimate		uekte, uaegte
natus	born		føde, født
nata	daughter born		datter født
natus	son born		sønn født
nepos	grandson, nephew, grandchild		sønnesønn, nevo or brorsønn-søstersønn barn, barn

GERMANIC LATIN AND DANISH TERMINOLOGY (Continued)

LATIN	ENGLISH	GERMAN SCRIPT	DANISH
neptis	niece granddaughter		brordatter, søster-datter,-datter,datter
nescitur	not known		ukendt
nomen	name		kalle, kaldet(named)
nothus (adj)	illegitimate		uekte, uaegte
Nuptiae	nuptials		brude, bryllups
secundae nuptiae	a second marriage		annen giftermål, annen ektskap
obitus	death		død
obstetrix	midwife		jordmor,giordmoder
orbatus	orphan		fødselshjelp
origo	birth, origin		byrd, fødsel
ortus	birth, origin		byrd, fødsel
pagus	village,district		landsby,distrikt
parens	parent		far,mor, føraeldre
parentes	parents		far,mor, føraeldre
parochia	parish		søgn, herred
parochianus	parishioner		som hører
partus	childbirth,labor		fødsel
pastor	pastor (eccles) shepherd		prest,sjèlesørger
pater	father		far, fader
paternalis	paternal		fader,faerlig
patrina	godmother		gudmor,gudmoder
patrinus	godfather		gudfar,gudfader
patrini	godparents		gudforelde
plutus	baptized,sprinkled		døbt

LATIN	ENGLISH	GERMAN SCRIPT	DANISH
pactio nuptialis	engagement		forlovelse
patruelis (m&F)	cousin		søskenbarn(firstcousin
proclamatio	decree, bann		forordning,bestemme, lysing, ekteskaps
progenitus	firstborn		førstefødt
proles	offspring, child (sex is not indicated by this word)		arkom
proavus	great grandfather		oldefar
proavia	great grandmother		oldemor
publicus	public		offentlig
puella	girl child		pike barn
puellus	boy child		gutt barn, dreng
puerpera	mother, newly delivered mother		mor
puerperium	childbirth		fødsel (birth)
purgatus	baptized, cleansed		døbt, døpt
ratio libitanae	death record		død registrere
religio	religion		religion, gudfryktig (devout)
reformate	of the reformed religion		omdanne religion
renatus	baptized, reborn		døpt, døbt
ristricus	step-father		- - -
senior	senior, older		eldre, eldst
senex	old man		gammel, el'd/gammel (extremely old)
sepultus	buried		begravet
socvusus	mother-in-law		swigermor
socer	father-in-law		swigerfar
solutus	unmarried, free from debt		ugift, gjeldfri

LATIN	ENGLISH	GERMAN SCRIPT	DANISH
soror	sister		søster
spinster	unmarried girl, or woman		ugift pige, or ugift kone
sponsa	bride, spouse, betrothed		brud, bruud, ektefelle aegtefelle
sponsale	betrothal		forlovelse, lysning
sponsalia	marriage banns		lyst til Aegteskab (published for marriage)
sponso	to marry		gifte
sponsus	groom, spouse betrothed		brudgom, bruudgom ektefelle, aegtefaelle
spurius	illegitimate		uekte, uaegte
superstes	surviving, still living		lengst lerende (survivor)
supervivo	to survive, outlive		overleve
susceptor	godparent		gudforelde
thorus	bed		seng, bed
ex legitimo thoro	legitimate		ektefødd, ekte
ex illegitimo thoro	illegitimate		uektefødd, uekte
tinctus	baptized, dipped		døbt, døpt
ultimus	last, final		lest, endelig
uterus	womb		mórsliv,
in utere	in the womb, not fully born		- - -
uxor	wife		hustru, dame, kone
vicinia	neighborhood		nàbolag, nàboskap

GERMANIC LATIN AND DANISH TERMINOLOGY (Continued)

LATIN	ENGLISH	GERMAN SCRIPT	DANISH
vicus	town, village		by, stad, kommune, landsby
videre	to see, witness		vitnes
vidus	widow		enke, aenke
viduus	widower		enkemand, aenkemann
villicus	village, townsman		landsbyboer
vir	man, husband		menneske, mann, ektefelle
virgo	unmarried girl.		jomfru
virtuosus	upright, honorable		hederlig
vita	life		liv, levetid (lifetime)
vixi	to live, be alive		leve, live, levende

ABREVIATIONS

p.v. - pudica virgo (a chaste young woman)
h.j. - honestus juvenis (a worthy young man)
l.c. - legitimi conjuges(a lawfully-wed couple)
M. - Maria
A. - Anna   An. Anna
J. - Johannes
hon.juf.-honestus juvenis (a worthy young man)
bapt. - baptized
fmts - famatus (well-known)
lgta - legitima (legitimate)
Nep - Nepomucenus - although this is a strange name, it was somewhat common in certain areas of Germany. You must remember that the scribes abreviated words and names which were common to them.

ADDITIONAL DANISH TERMS

afgift	duty, tax, rent
afkom	offspring
arving	heir
besidder	occupier
barneløs	childless
formynder	guardian
fraskildt	divorced
gods	estate
klog	wise, educated
kobstad	city
laegd	military district
laegdsruller	military levying
nyfødt	newborn
selvejer	owner, freeholder
skilsmisse	divorce

GLOSSARY OF ILLNESSES FOUND IN GERMAN CHURCH RECORDS

For those who are working in Roman Catholic Parish records, I wanted to give you a list of the Latin terms as well as the German terms. I am including the terminology in the old German script so that you may compare. For those who are working in the Schleswig-Holstein area during the Danish rule*, I have included the Danish word. This list is alphabetical according to the German word. On some, the old terms are placed beneath the word. I have gathered this material using mnay dictionaries. In some cases I could not find a single word, therefore, I have included several words that may give you a clue. No list is ever complete.

GERMAN	SCRIPT	ENGLISH	LATIN	DANISH
Abortus		abortion	abortio	abor't
Abtreibung		abortion	abortio	abor't
Abszeß Eiterbeule		abscess	abscessus	svull, svulst, byll
Abzehrung		consumption	consumptio	Tuberkulose
Alter		age, old age	aetas, senectus	utferdige udfaerdige (extremely old)
Altersschwäche Decrepitus Siech		weakness of old age stroke	infirmus aetas descrepitus involutio senilis	gammel (old)
Anfall, Schlagenfall				
Asthma Keist		asthma	asthmaticus (asthmatic)	as'tma
Aussatz Anmal, Muttermal Knollsucht-.Morve		leprosy syphilis	leprae, scabea, morbus requis	spedal'sk/het
äußerer Schaden		external damage violent death	externus damnum	u/daude
Auszehrung Lungenschwindsucht Brüstkranke Tabes, Korsen		consumption, phthisis (old age)	consumptio	tuberkulose
Bandwurm (see Nesselwurm)		tapeworm		ben'del/orm tin'te
Beulenpest (see Pest)		bubonic plague	pestilentia	pest byll, pest, plage, land'eplage, pestilens
Blähungen		flatulence		plaget av vind
Blatterrose		shingles		helvetes/d
Blattern		smallpox	pestis	pest
Blinddarment- zundung		appendicitis	appendix	blin'dtarm betennelse
Blutfluß Ruhr		hemorrhage	haemorrhoia	blo'ds/ tryrtning
Blutlauf Ruhr		hemorrhage	"	"
Blutgang Ruhr, Rotlauf		hemorrhage	"	"

*see footnote on page 20

GLOSSARY OF ILLNESSES FOUND IN GERMAN CHURCH RECORDS (Continued)

GERMAN	SCRIPT	ENGLISH	LATIN	DANISH
Blutsturz		violent hemorrage	sanguinem	vol'd/som
Blutvergiftung		blood poisoning	fundere (bleed)	blo'dstyrtning
Bräune		quinsy, angina		tonsilti's
Diphtherie				hal's/betenhelse
				halsbyll angina
Brand am Fuß		gangrene on the foot	- - - -	Koldbrann (?) av fot
Brechruhr		cholera	- - - -	Kolera
Broden		asthma	- - - -	astma
Bruchschaden		hernia	hernia	brokk'
Brustentzündung		pleurisy -bronchitis	pleuritis	brys't/hinne- beten'nelse
Brustbräune		heart attack	- - - -	hierteangribe
Brustfieber		bronchitis or inflammation of the chest	inflammatio pectus	beten'nelse av brys't
Brustkrämpfe		cramps, spasms convulsions of the chest	comprimere, spasmus, convulsio	kram'pe kram'pe/trekning
Brustwassersucht		dropsy of the chest	- - - -	vat'ter/sott
Cholera		cholera	- - - -	Ko'lera
Durchfall		diarrhea	proflurium	diar'e
Abweichen,Ruhr, Durchlauf				
Eiterbeule		abscess	absessus	svull'is, vul'st byll
Entkräftung		weakening, exhaus- tion,debilitation	infirmus, defat- igatio,debilis	svak/het (weakness svek'kelse
Epilepsie		epilepsy	morbus,comit- ialis	u't/trømming
Jammer,Bruch Brest,Falbel, Elend		epilepsy		fal'le/syke
Fallsucht		epilepsy	"	
Krenke				
Fehlgeburt		miscarriage	abortum fecere	dårligutfall u/hellj misfal
Faulfieber		putrid fever	putris febris	ratten feber
Fäule		cancer	cancer	kraeft
Fieber		fever	febris	feber
Beutelmann Schüttelfrost				
Fleckfieber		spotted fever	febris	tyfoid/feber
Typhus				ty'fus
Fleckenkrankeit		dry scab	aridus, crustus	tørr skörpe skur'v, skabb'

GERMAN	SCRIPT	ENGLISH	LATIN	DANISH
Flecktyphus (see Typhus) Petetchen		typhoid fever	---- febris	tørr skorpe skurv, skabb´
Flußfieber Influenza		rheumatic fever	febris	revma´tisk feber
Fraisen		convulsions,epilepsy, seizures, spasms	spasmus,convulsio	kram´pe
Frühgeburt		premature birth	praematurus partus	for ti´dlig forhas´ta
Gehirnschlag		cerebral apoplexy heart attack	cerebrum (brain)	hjernel/blødning apopleksi slag/anfal
Gelbsucht Aurogo,Icterus		jaundice	morbus regius icterus	gu`l/sott
Gelenkrheumatismus Gelenkentzündung, Gicht,Gliederkälte		arthritis		gik´t/brudden (arthritic) rheumatic
Geschwulst Blärr, Blarre, Pauken, Pfies		swelling or tumor, goiter	tumor	svul´men,svul´st Kver/sill,stru´ma (strangles)
Geschwür im Hals		ulcer in throat	ulcus, apostema jugulum	svull´, svelg, strupe hals
Gesichtsrose Antonius feuer		erysipelas		helvetes/eld
Gicht (St.)Andreas Krankheit Fluß . Nösch		arthritis, gout		gik´t/brudden (arthritic)
Gift		poisoning		gift
Gliederstopfung (see Schlagfluß)		apoplexy, stroke		slag/anfal
Gürtelrose		shingles		helvetes/eld
Häulige		croup		- - -
Hals abgeschnitten		throat cut	jugulum secare	hals skære snitt, hogg
Halsentzündung		throat infection	jugulum contagium	hals smitte
Halsschwindsucht		throat consumption	jugulum consumptio	besmittelelse
Hirnentzündung		brain infection	cerebrum contagium	hjern/smitte
hitziges Fieber		high fever (Typhoid)	calidus febris	het, heit, varm, feber
(schleichendes Fieber)		lingering fever	celer febris	hurtig/feber
Husten Keuchhusten		coughing	tussis (cough)	hoste (cough) stru`pe (choke)

GLOSSARY OF ILLNESSES FOUND IN GERMAN CHURCH RECORDS (Continued)

GERMAN	SCRIPT	ENGLISH	LATIN	DANISH
Influenza (Grippe) Krips, Bürzel,Kehlfluß, Kopfwustigkeit	*Influenza*	influenza	catarrh-us	influensa
innerliche Krankheit	*innerliche Krankheit*	internal disease	intestinus morbus	indre, innvortes sykdom
Ischias	*Ischias*	sciatica (inflammation of the sciatic nerve	inflammatio --- nervus	hoftegikt,
Keist	*Keist*	asthma	asthmaticus	astma
Keuchhusten	*Keuchhusten*	whooping cough	tussis	ki'k/hoste stru'pe/hoste (croup)
Kindbettfieber Mutterfrais	*Kindbettfieber*	childbed fever	infans lectus febris	bar'sel/feber
Kinderpocken Barpel, Berpel	*Kinderpocken*	chicken pox		vann'/kopper
Knochenfraß Busse,Krebs	*Knochenfraß*	caries cancer		Kronisk
Knochenkrebs	*Knochenkrebs*	bone cancer	os cancer	beinbetennelse bein kraeft
Kolik grimme Mutter,Kneif Bauchgrimmer,Koolke	*Kolik*	colic		
Kopfwasser	*Kopfwasser*	hydrocephalus		vann pähjernen ?
Krämpfe Bangigkeit der Kinder Klamm,Kontraktur	*Krämpfe*	cramps, spasms, convulsions	comprimere, spasmus convulsio	krampe
Krätze Juck,Scharre	*Krätze*	scabies (sever itch)	scabies, pruriog	fnatt', skabb'
Krebs Busse,Knochenfraß Faüle,Krebsge, Schwür	*Krebs*	cancer	cancer	Kraeft
Kropf Balbina Kelch	*Kropf*	goiter		stru'ma
Krupp	*Krupp*	croup - diptheria	- - - -	diferitis
langwierige Krankheit	*langwierige Krankheit*	prolonged illness	extendere morbus	forlenge sy'kdomtegn prolongeresyk dom
Lustfeuche	*Lustfeuche*	syphillis	---	---
Lungenentzündung	*Lungenentzündung*	pneumonia		lunge/beten nelse lunge/brann
Lungenkatarrh	*Lungenkatarrh*	pulmonary disease	pulmoneus, pulmonarius	lunge sykdom lunge/urt
Lungenschwind- sucht	*Lungenschwindsucht*	consumption, tuberculosis	morbus	
Lungensucht	*Lungensucht*	"	"	"
(Lungenlähmung	*Lungenlähmung*	"	"	"

GLOSSARY OF ILLNESSES FOUND IN GERMAN CHURCH RECORDS (Continued)

GERMAN	SCRIPT	ENGLISH	LATIN	DANISH

Magenkatarrh
  Magen, hitziger,
  Kalter
		gastritis	stomachus
			pertinens
				Ma`ge/katärr
				mavesår(gast.ulcer

Magenschwäche		stomach disease	stomachus morbus	mave sykdom
Mandelbräune Mandelentzündung		tonsillitis		
Masern Blatter,Flecken rote,Kinderblattern		measles	morbilli	mes`linger,   kri`lle,tin`te   kreg`de
Milzverhärtung		anthrax	---	---
Nervenfieber Typhus		nervous fever typhoid	trepidus febris, --	feber, tyfoid
Nesselwurm (see Bandwurm)		tapeworm	--	bendelorm tin`te
Pedchien		typhotic fever	---- febris	tyfoid/feber ty`fus

Pest
  Contagio, Kog(e).
  Düsel. Emmissio.
  Seucht
		plague	pestis,
			pestilentia
				pest, plage, byll

Pocken
  Blattern,Feuer,,
  Hautausschlag
		pox, smallpox		kop`per (small)

Räude
  Schnupfer,Katarrh,
  Aussatz
		dry scab		skabb`, skurv

Röteln		German measles	----morbilli	mes`linger
Rachenbräune		diptheria		
Rheuma		rheumatism	------	reumatism

Ruhr
  Blutfluf, Blutlauf,
  Dysenteria, rote
  Ruhr
		dysentery	dysenteria	dysenteri

Samenfluß		gonorrhea	--	--
Scharlachfieber Riesel,Scarlatum		scarlet fever	coccum febris	ska`rlaks/feber skarla`gens/feber
Schlaganfall Anfall , Freischlein		cerebral apoplexy (stroke)	cerebrum(brain) ---	jkerne/blødning apopleksi

Schlagfluß
  Apoplexie,Fluf
  Freischlein
		apoplexy,
		apoplectic
		stroke
			"	apopleski
				sla`g/anfall

Schleimfieber		typhus	typhus	sli`met feber
Schwachsinn		feeblemindedness	infirmus, debilis	våk, sva`k
Schwäche Debilitas,Dissolu- tio, Gravitas		weakness	infirmitas, debilitas senilis	sva`k/het sy`kelig/het

33

GLOSSARY OF ILLNESSES FOUND IN GERMAN CHURCH RECORDS (Continued)

GERMAN	SCRIPT	ENGLISH	LATIN	DANISH
Schwämme Krebs		fungus	fungus	---
Schwindsucht Beuschel,Dörrsucht, Glieder,Stopfung, Phtisis,Tabes,Darre		consumption asthma	consumptio	fortaerling(?) (tuberkulo´se)
Stickfluß Asthma Brustwassersucht		choking catarrh angina pectoris	suffocatio --	kve´le, stoppe (choke) katarr
Stickhusten Stickfraisen Kramph hafter		whooping cough	----- tusis	kik/hoste stru´pe/huste
Syphillis Franzosen,Aussatz Maselsucht		syphillis	---	---
Typhus Düsel,Pest,Faulfieber Gallenfieber Schleimfieber		typhus	typhus	ty´fus
Tobsucht Wutanfall Zornkrankheit		raving madness	furi osus insania	split´tende
Tuberkulose		tuberculosis		
Unbestimmte Krankheit		undefined disease	infinitus morbus	ubestem´melig (undefinable)
Unterleibstyphus		Typhoid fever	typhus	sykdom typhus
Vergiftung		poisoning	- --	- - -
Wasserkopf (see Kopfwasser)		hydrocephalus	---	---
Wassersucht Hydrops		dropsy	hydropicus	vatersott
Weichselzopf		matted hair in- fested by lice	---	lus,
Windpocken Drösebleder		chickenpox	---	vann`/kopper
Wochenbettfieber		childbed fever	infans lectus febris	bar`sell feber
Würmer		worms	vermiculosus vermis	ha orm
Wurmfieber Darmkatarrh		typhus	vermis febris	orm feber
Zahnfleisch- entzündung		gingivitis	---	tannkjøtt
Zahnfieber		"		"
Zahnung		teething	-----	-----
Ziegenpeter		mumps	---	kus´ma
Zuchung		cramps, convulsion	spasmus convulsio	krampe

I hope this will give you some clues

I wanted to give you a working list of occupations. However, there is no way I could give you a complete list. I have not included some of the modern day occupations, since you will be working with old records in most cases. A good German-English dictionary should be in your library. Those working in Roman Catholic records may want to have a Latin-English dictionary.

German occupations are always preceded by masculine "der" or feminine "die". I have eliminated these in order to save space. I have included the occupation written in script to help you identify the word.

Knowing the occupation may help you identify the ancestor when there are 8 or 10 men in the same parish or village, in the same time frame with the same name. Since occupations stayed within families, it may also help you to find other generations. Keep in mind that some may have apprenticed with an uncle or other relative and that would give you additional members of a family.

For those working with Roman-Catholic records, I have included the Latin word. For those working in the Schleswig-Holstein area during the Danish rule, you may find the record written in Danish. (See footnote on page 14)

Since you will be working from the German to the English, the list is alphabetical according to the German word. I have gathered this material using many dictionaries. In some cases I could not find a single word, therefore, I have included several words that may give you a clue.

GERMAN	SCRIPT	ENGLISH	LATIN	DANISH
Ackermann Ackerwirt Ackersmann		husbandman, farmer small farmer	agricola arator colonus	husmand jordbruker bonde (peasant)
Adeliger Edelmann		nobleman	vir nobilis	adelsmann
Aderlasser		barber-surgeon (bleeder of veins)	minutor, pflebotomarius	
Altbürger		Full citizen	————	————
Altbürgermeister		former mayor	prior praefectus urbi	forrige- borgmester
Amman		bailiff, magistrate		
Amtmann		magistrate	magistratus	ørrighetsperson fredsdommer
Amtmann		provost warden	custos, ammann, granarius, officialis	domprost opsynsmann
Amtsknecht		messenger servant	famulus	tjener tiener
Amtsverwalter		administrator	administrator	bestyrer administrator
Anbauer		peasant	————	————
Anstreicher Tüncher Weissbinder		painter (house)	pictor	maler
Anwalt		lawyer, guardian	eustos jurisconsultus praeses (m&f) defensor	advokat

GERMAN	SCRIPT	ENGLISH	LATIN	DANISH
Apotheker		pharmacist	apothecarius pharmacopola	apotek ? (pharmacy)
Arbeiter (m) Abeiterin (f)		worker, laborer	operarius laborius	arbejdsmand arbejdsmann
Arbiter Schöffe		juror (lay)	---------	jurymand
Archäologe		archaeologist	antiquitatis	arkeolog
Architekt		architect	architectus	arkitekt
Archivar		archivist	tabularus	arkivar (dokumenter)
Armer		poorman, beggar	pauper	fattig, tigger
Arzt		physician	medicus	laege
Astrologe		astrologer	astrologus	astrolog
Aufseher Büttel		supervisor	apparitor guardianus	tilstnsførende
Ausländer		foreigner	peregrinus	fremmed
Auswanderer		emigrant	emigrans	utvandrer
Bader		barber, surgeon	barbarius chirurgus	barberer, kirurg
Bäcker Bäckermeister Bachmann Böck		baker master baker	pistor, panifex talemetarius	bager, bager- mester
Bäckergeselle		baker, journeyman	pistor opifex	baker, baker/ jaere
Bamutter		midwife	obstetrix	jordmor
Bankier		banker	argentarius numnularius	bankier
Barbier		barber	tonsor	barberer
Bartscherer		barber	tonsor	barberer

GERMAN	SCRIPT	ENGLISH	LATIN	DANISH

Bauer
 Buhmann
		farmer	colonus, paur
			  agricola, rurensis
			   rusticus
				agerdyrker
				bonde,gaard-
				   bruger

Baumeister		master builder,
		  construction
		  supervisor
		  architect
			aedifcator
			  superare
			  construére
			  architectus
				konstruktion-
				  tilsynsførende
				
				  arkitekt

Baumgärtner		gardener	hortulanus olitor	gartner
Beamter		official	minister, magistrus	officiel
Beck(er)		baker	pistor	bager
Berater		counselor, advisor	consiliarius,consultor	radgiver
Bernsteindreher		amber turner	paternoster————	– – –

Beruf
 Gewerbe
		occupation, trade,
		  or profession
			–	erhverve,
				  stilling
				  (position)
				  handtering
				  (trade)

Bergmann Hauer		miner	metallicus, fossor	bergmann gruvearbeider

Besitzer		owner, proprietor,
		  or possessor
			dominus,
			  possessor
				besitter

Besenbinder		broom maker	virgulator	gyrelfabrikant lynfabrikant
Bettler		beggar	mendicus, stripus	tigger, betler
Bierbrauer		beer brewer	cerevisiarius, coctor, tabernarius	brygmester
Biersieder		beer distiller	cerevisiarius	brennevinsbrenner
Bilderhändler		picture merchant	iconpola	billede grosser
Bildhauer		sculptor	sculptor scalptor	billedhugger
Bildschnitzer		wood carver	lignum caelator	skog skaere ? forskjaere
Bischof		Bishop	——————	Biskop
Binder		binder	ligarus	bokbinder ,binde
Blattgoldschläger		hammers gold leaf	practeator	
Bleicher		bleacher	albator, candidarius	bleikner
Bleigießer		lead smelter	plumbum fundére	blyhytte- arbeider
Bortenmacher Posamentierer		lace maker	– – –	kniplingmaker

GERMAN	SCRIPT	ENGLISH	LATIN	DANISH
Böttcher Bekemaker, Einleger		cooper barrelmaker or repairer	viego, vietor, doliarius, ligator	bødker
Bote Träger Brauer Briefbote		messenger brewer mailman	nuntius, baiulus, tabellarius, tabellio, gerulus tabularius	bud postmann
Briefträger		mail carrier	tabularius, lator litterarum	postmann
Brücken zöllner		bridge, toll collector	ponticus, poritor exactor	bridge avgift samler
Brunnenbauer		constructor of wells	putearius	kjelde bygge-
Brunnenmeister		master of the pump room	aquilex	Kjelde tillsynsmann
Bürstenmacher		Brushmaker	- - -	børstenbinder
Buchbinder		book binder book maker	bibliopegus	bokbinder bokfabricant
Buchdrucker		printer	imprimerer	boktrykker bogtrykker
Buchhändler Bösselmacher		book dealer	librarius, bibliopola concinnator librorum	bokhandler boghandler
Buchhalter		bookkeeper	calculator actuarius	bokholder bogholder
Buchmaler		book illustrator	- - -	- - -
Büdner		stall keeper	- - -	parket holde-
Buchsenmacher Buchsenschmied		rifle maker gunsmith	bombardarius	snappebort rifle fabrikant børsmaker
Buhmann Bauer Bürge		sponsor	sponsor	kausjonist (endorser)
Bürger		citizen burgher	civis burgensis	borger
Bürgermeister Ratsherr		mayor	consiliarius, magister civium, consul, praetor	borgmester
Büttel Waibel		jailer, bailiff	bidellus, lictor	gard offisiell
Büttner		cooper	cadus fabricator	Tønne fabrikator Tønner

38

OCCUPATIONS AND TITLES (Continued)

GERMAN	SCRIPT	ENGLISH	LATIN	DANISH
Burgmann		castle steward	castrensis (of estate)	borghovmester
Cantor, Kantor		Choirmaster, organist Chanter church liturgy church music dir.,	cantator	kor------sanger
Chirurg		surgeon	chirurgus	kirurg
Corporal		corporal	- - -	- - -
Dachdecker		thatcher roof tiler	tector, contegulator	halmtekker tak teg/ tekker
Dechanat, Dekan Probst		dean (church or university)	decanus	dekan
Deserteur		deserter	- - -	ørken- ?
Dichter		poet	poeta	digter
Dieb		thief	fur	tyv, tyfr
Dienstbote		domestic servant	- - -	- - -
Dienstmädchen		servant girl	famella (f)	tjenerpige
Dienerin		servant (female)	ancilla (f)	tjenestepige
Diener		servant (Male)	famellus (m) famulus	tjenestepike
Doktor		learned man	doktor	doktor
Dragoner		dragoon	- - -	- - -
Drescher		turner, thresher	tritor, dreyer, tomeator, tomio	dreier
Drahtzieher		wire drawer	- - -	- - -
Drucker		printer	impressor, presser	boktrykker
Durchreisender		stranger, transient	advena, pereg- rinas	fremmed forbigående
Ebentürer Juwelenhändler		jewel merchant	- - -	smykker- guldsmed
Edelmann		nobleman	vir nobilis	adelsmann
Eigengärtner		independent gardner	- - -	- - -
Einnehmer Rentmeister		collector	aerarius praefec- tus, imbursator, aerarius quaestor	samler
Einlieger		landless farm laborer	------	------
Einwohner		inhabitant	incola (m & f)	indbygger

39

OCCUPATIONS AND TITLES (Continued)

GERMAN	SCRIPT	ENGLISH	LATIN	DANISH
Eisengießer		iron founder	ferreus conditor	jernstøper
Eisenhändler		ironmonger (dealer)	ferreus mercator	jernhandler jernkremmer
Eisenschmelzermeister Frischmeister		iron smelting meister	- - -	- - -
Eisenschmied		blacksmith	ferrarius	smed
Elektriker		electrician	- - -	elektriker
Erbpächter Erbbauer		hereditary tenant	- - -	- - -
Erzgraber		ore miner (metalminer)	aes fosser metallicus	malmarbeider
Erzieher		educator	praeceptor magister	pedagog
Essigbrauer		vinegarmaker	- - -	eddikemaker
Eßigbrauer Estrichmacher		flooring, pavement, stone floor makers	- - -	gulvmaker fortov
Fähnrich		officer, cadet ensign, midshipman	- - -	officer,
Fahnentrager		flag bearer	vexillum bajulus	flagindehaver
Fahrmann		ferryman	portitor, navector	ferjemann
Färber		dyer	tinctor, infector, colorator	farvere
Faktor		manager, super-visor	curator procurarer	bestyrer tilsynsførende
Faßbinder		cooper	cuparius	kobber
Feilenhauer		file maker	lima fabricator?	tråd, metall-tråd, filer
Feldhüter		field watchman field warden	ager vigil ager custos	mark jorde vector mark opsyns-mand vekter
Feldmesser Erdtrichsmesser		surveyor	agrimensor	oppsynsmann
Feldwebel		sergeant	optio	sersjant
Festbäcker		rye bread baker	- - -	? brød bager
Feuerwerker		explosives expert maker of fire-works	fragor (explo-sion) accendere (fire)	eksplosiv ørd ekspert fyrverkeri
Fischer		fisherman	piscator	fisker, fidsker
Fischhändler		fishmonger (dealer)	piscator mercator	fisker klop-mann (merchant)

GERMAN	SCRIPT	ENGLISH	LATIN	DANISH
Flaschenmacher		bottle maker	ampularius	flasker
				flask fabrikan
Fleischbeschauer		meat inspector	caro curator	køds inspektør
Fleischer		butcher	carnarius,	slagter
Metzger			macellarius, mactator	
Fleischhauer				
Flieger		flyer		flyger
Flickschneider		mending tailor	reparare vestitor	repare're
			textor	skraedder
Fliesenmacher		Tile stove maker	_ _ _	
Kacheler				
Flößer		raftsman	ratis (raft)	flåteforer
Fluchting		refugee, deserter	------	--------
Förster		forest ranger	forestarius	forstmann
Folterknecht		executioner (hangman) torturer	carnifex crucia toritortor	sharpretter bøddel
Fourier		quartermaster	castrorum praefectus	kvartermester
Fräulein		miss, young lady	virgo	frøken
Freibauer		independent peasant, freeholder	dominus	fribonde
Freiherr		Baron	-----	-------
Fremder		stranger, foreigner	adrena	fremmed
Friseur		barber	tonsor	barber
Fürst		prince	regulus, regis filius	prins
Fuhrmann		coachman, wagoner	carrucarius, auriga, vector plaustrarius	karétkusk kjører - kjørekar
Karrenzieher				
Heinzler				
Gardist		guardsman	aedituus, custos (guardian, guard)	vaktmann vagtmand
Gärtner		gardner	hortulanus, ortulanus	gartner
Gastwirt		innkeeper	hospes, caupo	krovaert
Wirt				
Leitgeb				

GERMAN	SCRIPT	ENGLISH	LATIN	DANISH
Gaukler		magician vagabond minstrel	magus, ioculator vagabundus fidicen	tryllekunstner omstreifende skald, sanger
Geistlicher		clergyman	sacerdos, clericus	praest
Geischelmacher Peitschenmacher		whip maker	-- --	piskmaker
Geldeinnehmer		money collector money lender	faenerator	pengesamler vekseler (money agent)
Gemeindediener		community messenger	nuntius civitas	samfund bud
Gemusegartner		vegetable gardner	macellum hortulanus	markedsgartner
Gemusehandler Grönhöker Moshake		grocer- vegetable green grocer	olitor	købmand grønthandler
Gerber Weissgerber Lederer, Rotgerber		tanner	cerdo, albicerdo tauer	garver
Gerichts- beisitzer		associate judge	judex	omgas dommer
Gericht		Court	------	dom
Gerichts- diener		servant in the court	forum famulus	tjenergard
Gerichts- schoffe		juror	consessor	dommer bisitter
Gerichts- schreiber		clerk in the court	forum clericus forum scriba	kontorist tennisbane
Gerichts- verwandter		court official	forum publicus	tennisbane (officiel)
Geschäft		trade, business	negotium	erhverv. forretning
Geselle, Lehrling		journeyman, apprentice	opfex	svenn-svend
Gesellherr Hilfgeistlicher		assistant to clergyman	discipulus	laeregutt(dreng)
Gesetzgeber		legislator law maker	legumlator	lovgiver
Geschäftsmann		businessman	negotiator	forret'nings/folk
Gewerbe		trade, occupation	---	forret'nings drivende beskaeftigelse
Gewürzkrämer		grocer, dealer in spices	Imber, speciarius	krvdderi grosserer

GERMAN	SCRIPT	ENGLISH	LATIN	DANISH
Gießer		founder, caster, molder	- - -	støper, kaster
Gilde		guild	collegium sodalitas	gild
Glaser		glazier, glass-man	vitriarius	glaserer polerer skive
Glasarbeiter		glassmaker glassblower	vitrarius vitreus inflarer	glasmester glassblässer
Glashandler		glass handler	- - -	glasshandler
Glasmaler Glasschriver		glass painter (stained glass)	vitreus pector	flasmaler
Glockengießer		bell founder	(large) campana fundator (small) tininnabulum fundator	klokke støper ?
Glöckner Küster		sexton, bellringer	campanarius pulsant	klokker
Glufenmacher Nadelmacher		needle/pin maker	- - - -	nål/knappenål maker
Goldschmied Edelschmied		goldsmith	bractearius, durifaber aurifaber-aurifex	guldsmith
Graf Pfalzgraf		Count Earl	Comes, comes palatinus	greve jarl
Greis Greisin		old man old woman	senex - - -	gammel mann gammel kvinde
Greisler		Grütz or groats dealer	- - -	- - -
Grenadier		grenadier infantryman	peditatus	infanteri-mann
Grobschmied		blacksmith	ferrarius	smed
Groß-Herzog Großherzog		grand duke	grandux	storhertug
Groß-Herzogin Großherzogin		grand duchess	grandduca	stor-hertuginne
Gürtler Gürtelmacher		beltmaker	cingularius, funicularius, zonarius	baeltefabrikant belte
Gutspachter		lessee of estate	conductor fundus	bo oppsitter (lease holder)
Gütler		inhabitant of small farm	- - -	- - -
Häcker Häker		vine grower or landworker small farmer	- - -	vin vorkse ?
Händler Höke		dealer, trader, merchant	mercator	forhandler, grosser, klopmann
Hachmeister		overseer of hunting grounds	- - - -	- - - -

GERMAN	SCRIPT	ENGLISH	LATIN	DANISH
Hackenbüdner		hook seller	- - -	- - -
Halbbauer		half-share farmer semi-farmer	dimida agricola semi agricola	halv bonde
Hammerschmied		blacksmith	ferrarius **malleator.**	smed
Handel		trade	- -	erhverv
Handschuhmacher Beutler		glove maker	**chirothecarius,** gantier,pellarius	handsker handskemaker
Handwerker		craftsman	artifex, **opifex**	hendighet handverker
Harfner		musician, harpist	musicus, **harpator** psaltes	musician
Harmaker Haardechenmacher		horsehair quilt maker		
Hauer Bergmann Minierer		miner's wages miner	metallicus fosser	minearbejder
Hauptmann		captain	**aedilis**	kaptajn
Haubenmacher		milliner	- - -	modehandler
Haubenschmied		helmet maker	- - -	- - -
Hausdiener		house servant	domus famulus(m) domus famula(f)	hustjener
Hausgenosse		household member, fellow lodger	- - -	- - -
Hausierer Spielmann Gängler		peddler	venditor, **abenteurer,** **tallierer**	høker
Häusler Keuschler		cottager landless laborer	servus (serf)	boelsmand
Hausmeister		caretaker	curarer	oppsynsmann
Hebamme Wehmutter		midwife	obstetrix	jordmor fødselshjelper
Heger		game-warden	- - -	vildtopsyns mann
Hefesieder Gerbensieder		yeastmaker	- - -	= - -
Heizer		stoker, fireman	- - -	fyrbøter,brannmann
Helmmacher		helmet maker	- - -	- - -
Hemdenmacher Hembder Pfaidler		shirtmaker	**indusiarius,**	skjortemaker skjortefab- rikant
Henker		executioner torturer	tortor, **carnifex** (hangman)	bød'del
Herr		master, lord, Lord	magister	herre

GERMAN	SCRIPT	ENGLISH	LATIN	DANISH
Herzog		duke	dux	hertug
Herzogin		duchess	duxa	hertugin'ne

Heuerling
  Mieter or Mietling
		tenant, hireling,
		  day laborer
			– – –	lejer

Hexe		witch	venefica	hekse
Hiepenbäcker Oblatenbäcker		communion wafer	– – –	– – –
Hilfsgeistlicher		assistant clergyman	capellanus	Kapelan,cappelan
Hintersaß Grundsasse		small land holder	– – –	– – –
Hirt(e) (m)		herdsman, shepherd (also pastor)	pastor, opilio	hyrde (m)
Hirtin (f)		herder female	– – –	hyrdinne (f)
Höfling		courtier		
Höriger		bondsman – serf	pertinens homo	– – –
Holzflößer		raftsman	– – –	– – –
Holzhändler		lumber merchant	scruta mercator	tømmerhandler

Holzhauer		woodcutter	lignator ?
			  (woodmann)
				vedhogger
				  braendenhugge

Holzschuhmacher		maker of wooden shoes	– – –	– – –
Holzschuhhändler		wooden shoe merchant	– – –	– – –
Holztrogmacher		wooden trough maker	– – –	– – –
Hopfenbauer		hop grower	saltus cultor	humle dryker
Hofmuttersmann Milchviehzüchter		milk cow breeder	– – –	– – –
Honighandler		honey dealer		honning grosserer
Hornist		horn player	cornutibicen	hornbläser
Hüfner		farmer	agricola	bonde,gaardbruger
Hufschmied		blacksmith	– – –	– – –
Huf und Waffenschmied		blacksmith and weaponsmaker	– – –	– – –
Hutmacher		hat maker	pilearius, pileo	hattemager

Hure
  Dirne,
  Mätresse
		prostitute
		  (kept) mistress
			meretrix, proca
			  – – –
				– – –

Imker Zeidler, Beutner		bee keeper	apiarius	biebesitler
Inwohner		inhabitant	incola	indbygger
Jagdgehilfe		hunter's assistant	– – –	– – –
Juwelenhändler Ebentürer		jewel merchant	– – –	– – –
Kärcher		coachman	currus, carruser	kjører, kus'k

Kämmerer		chamberlain – high
		  court digitary
			cancellarius
			  (chancellor)
				kammerherre

Kachelmacher
  Töpfer
		tile stove maker	gemmagenum,
			  ollarius
				– – –

OCCUPATIONS AND TITLES (Continued)

GERMAN	SCRIPT	ENGLISH	LATIN	DANISH
Kammerdiener		butler, valet	promus	kjellermester
Kalkbrenner		lime burner	calx urerer	kalk brenner lind brenner
Kammacher Hornrichter		comb maker	– – –	kammager
Kannengießer Kandler Kantengießer		pewterer	stannarius	blikkenslager
Kantor, Cantor		singer, choir dir., churh. music dir., organist, chanter church liturgy	cantator	sanger
Kanzleibeamter		chancery clerk	– – –	kanslerretten
Kaplan		chaplain	sacellanus, altarista	prest
Käsehändler		cheese-monger (dealer)	casier, tyrupola	osthandler ostkremmer
Käthner, Kötter Koter		small farmer	servus	boelsmand
Kaufmann		merchant	negotiant mercator	handelsmann kløpmann
Kellerein- verwalter Kellermeister		keeper of the wine celler	promocondus	knaeldermester
Kellner Diener Butteler		waiter	caniparius, credenzer	tjener
Kerkermeister		jailer, gaoler	ergastularius	faengselmester
Kerzenzieher Kerzengiefer		candlemaker	lychnopoeus	stearninlts fabrikant
Kessler Kesselschmied Beckenschlager		boilermaker tinker	abenarius farber pelvarius	dampkjele kjeleflikker
Kettenschmied		chainsmith		kaedesmed
Kielfederschaber Posenschaber				
Kindermädchen		nurse for children	amme nutrire in- fantium	barnepleierske barnpike
Kirchenpfleger Kirchenälster Kirchenvorsteher		Church warden church treasurer, head trustee	ecclesia custos	kirketjener
Kirchenschöffe		church assessor	ecclesia consessor	kirke dommer
Kistenmacher		crate maker chest or trunk maker	cistarus	pakk-korg fabrikant tremmekasse
Kisten-Truhen- macher		cabinetmaker trunkmaker	– – –	møbelsnekker

GERMAN	SCRIPT	ENGLISH	LATIN	DANISH
Klempner Spengler Beschlägemacher		plumber	fibulator	blyarbeider beytekker
Konig		King	Rex	konge
Konig"in		Queen	Regina	dronning
Kossät, Kossath		Cottager	------	-----
Knappe		squire	amiger	våpendrager
Knecht		servant	ancilla (f) familas (m)	tjener
Knopfmacher Knäufler		button maker	bulla fabricant	knapper fabrikant
Koch (m)		cook	cocus, coquus (m) garcifer	kokke (m)
Köbler"		small farmer	servus	boelsmand
Kochin (f)		cook	coqua (f)	kokkelpike (f)
Köhler"		charcoal burner	carbonarius	traekul dranner
Korbmacher Mandenmacher		basket maker wickerworker	sportularius	kurvfletning (wicker worker)
Korbflechter Kürbenzeiner		basket weaver	corbo	kurv/vaever kurvarbeid
Kornhausverwalter		granary administrator	horreum administrator	korn/kammer ?
Kornmesser		grain measurer		kornmaler
Kötter, Koter Käthner'"		small farmer	servus	boelsmand
Kramer		peddler, shopkeeper	merzler, fragner, actionarius, institor	- - - købmand
Krankenpfleger		nursing orderly (m)	- - -	syke/passer
Krankenschwester		female nurse	nutrix	syke/pleierske
Krankenwärter"		male nurse	aegrotarius	sykepleirer
Kruger or Kroeger		inn keeper	hospes	krovaert
Kuchenba"cker		confectioner	crustularius, cupendinarius	konditor
Küfer," Kübler Böttcher, Kupfer Weissbinder",Kiefer		cooper	viego, vietor, dolarius, cuparius, tunnarius, aeravius	bødker
Kurschner		furrier	pelzer, pelvifex pellificator,	buntmaker buntmager
Kuster" Glöckner		sexton church caretaker or custodian	aedituus campanarius	Kirche oppsyns-mann

OCCUPATIONS AND TITLES (Continued)

GERMAN	SCRIPT	ENGLISH	LATIN	DANISH
Kuhhirt (m)		cowherder (m)	domare pastor	kokyrde
Kuhhirtin (f)		cowherder (f)	- - -	vokter
Kunkelmacher " Spinnenrockenmacher		spinningwheel maker	- - -	- - -
Kunstler		skilled workman	faber, opifex	dyktig arbeider
Kürschner or Kursener Pelzhändler		furier	- - -	pels——
Kunsthändler "		art dealer	ars mercator	kunst
Kunsttischler		cabinet maker	armarium fabricant	møbelsnekker
Kupferdrucker		copperplate printer	- - -	kopperplate
Kupferschmied		coppersmith	- - -	koppersmed
Kupferstecher		copperplate engraver, etcher	**chalcographus**	kobergravere
Küster,Opfermann		sexton, parish clerk	- - -	- -
Kutscher Kärcher Fuhrmann		coachman	currus, carruser	kjører kus'k
Laternenmacher Luchtenmacher		lantern maker	- - -	lygtemager
Läufer		messenger	nuntius	bud
Laier **Laie**		layman **lay woman**	- - -	lekmann
Landmann Landwirt		farmer	agricola colonus	bonde (peasant)
Landmesser		surveyor	agrimensor metator	land/maler
Landstreicher **Bettler**		tramp	**ribaldus, gailer,** circulator, girator	vandre
Lastträger " Omenträger Lederhändler		porter leather dealer	janitor, ostiarius ostiarius	drager laeder - - -
Lehnsmann		vassal (slave)	servus	vasall
Lehrer (m)		teacher, educator	magister	laerer
Lehrerin (f)		teacher	magistra	laererinne

GERMAN	SCRIPT	ENGLISH	LATIN	DANISH
Lehrmeister		master of trade	superare mercator	mesterav-handler
Leibeigener		serf, bondsman	servus, verna,	livegen,slave
Leichenbediener		undertaker	adictus	kausjonist
Leiermann		organ-grinder (hurdy-gurdy)	organum ???	lire-kasse-mann
Leinenweber				
Leinweber		linen weaver	linifex,	lerretsvever
Lachenweber			linearius	
Leutnant		lieutenant	legatus praefectus	løytnant
Leutpriester		lay priest	??? priest	legge prest
Lodenmacher		maker of coarse	laneus texer	uldemager
Lodenweber		woolen cloth	(wollen weave) lodex culcitarius	
Magd		maidservant	ancilla, **obsequa**	tjenestepige
Magister		schoolmaster	ludimagister ludimoderator	lae`remester
Makler		middle man	mereidius	mellemstemand
Meier				
Niederrichter		overseer, rent collector, steward, keeper of a milk farm	curator, **villicus**	- - -
Maler		painter, artist, decorator	pictor artifex exornator	malerkunster
Mälzer		beer distiller	**brasiator**	brennesvins-brenner
Malzmüller		malt miller		
Marketender		canteen proprietor	caupona castrensis possessor(owner)	marketenteri
Mattenwirker				
Matzenmacher		unleavened bread maker	- - -	- - -
Maurer		mason bricklayer	**cementarius, murarius,**macio	Murer
Mehlhändler		flour trader	- - -	melgrocerer
Mehlker		meal man		
Meister		master,expert	superare, peritus	mester
Messingschmied		brassworker		
Messerschmied		cutler,sword furb-	**messor, metator**	- - -
Schwertfeger		sword furbisher	auric(h)alcifaber	
Metzger				
Fleischer		butcher	**lanio, carnifex,**	slagter
Schlager			**carnarius**	

GERMAN	SCRIPT	ENGLISH	LATIN	DANISH

Mieter
  Mietsmann
		tenant, lodger,
		  hirer
			conductor,
			  inquilinus
				innehaver
				  besitter

Milchhändler Milchmagd		milkman milkmaid	- - -	maelkemand meiereske

Milchwerkschaft,
  Molkerei
  Milchteller
		dairy	cella lacteria	meieri

Möbeltischler
  "
Müller
		cabinet maker
		  furniture maker
		miller
			supellex fabricant
			
			molitor,pistor,
			  molendarius
				møbel/snekker
				
				møller

Mündel		orphan	orbus	foreld/laus
Mundschenk Münzschneider		butler, cupbearer coin or medal stamp cutter	promus,pocillator monetarius	kjellermeister montmager ?

Musiker
  Musikant
  Geiger
		musician	musicus	musiker
				  musikant

Musketier
  Carbiner
		musketeer,
		  infantry
		  soldier
		  knight
			peditatus
			
			miles
			eques
				musketére
				
				soldat
				ridder

Nabenschmied		cartwright wheelwright	- - -	hjul- - ?
Nach.twächter		night watchman	nox vigil	natt vector

Nadelmacher
  Nättler,Noldner
		needle or pin maker	- - -	nål or knappenål-
				  mager

Nagelschmied		nail smith	**calvarius**	neglsmed

Näherin
  Näher
		seamstress,
		  dressmaker
			**neygerin, netor,
			  netrix**
				sy/dame
				dameskraed-
				  derinde

Notar		notary civil lawyer official scribe	scriba jurisconsultus civilis scriba	notarius
Oberkoch		master chef	coquus dominus	mesteroverkok
Oberpfarrer		rector		overhode minister

Oblatenbäcker
  Hiepenbäcker
  "
		communion wafer baker	- - -	

Obstverkaufer		fruit salesman	fructus venditor	fruktexpedien

GERMAN	SCRIPT	ENGLISH	LATIN	DANISH
Ochsenknecht		cowherder	domare pastor	vok´ter hjurings (m hjuring/tentag
Ohlenmacher		potter	euler	pottemager
Orgelbauer Kunstmeister		organ builder	organum structor	orgelbygger
Orleymacher		clock maker	horologiarius	uhrmager
Ortsfremder		stranger	advena, peregrinus	fremmed
Pächter		lessee, tenant	**reddituarius, arrendator**	bo oppsitter
Papierhandler		paper trader	charta mercator	papir hand/ler naerings- drivende
Paternostermacher		Rosarymaker (amber)	----------	
Papiermacher Papiermüller		papermaker	**bapirifex**, chartarius molend(in)arius papyriacus	papirmøller (papermiller)
Pauker		drummer	tympanista	trommer
Pedell		servant	famulus	tjener
Pergamentmacher Permeider		parchmentpaper maker	permiter	- - -
Perücken- macher		wigmaker	**capillamentarius**	parykkmaker
Pfandnehmer		pawnbroker	pignevator	pante/laner
Pfannenschmied		pot or pan maker	pastellator	pandesmed
Pfarrer Priester		minister, pastor, priest	pastor, antistes, **parochus, plebanus**	minister, prest praest
Pfarrkind		parishioner	- - -	
Pfeffer- handler		pepper trader	piper mercator	peber-naerings- drivende
Pfeifenmacher Piepker		pipe maker	- - -	pibemager
Pfeifer Flötenbläser		piper	**fistulator**	piper
Pferdeknecht		ostler stableman, groom	curare	spillemann stallkar

GERMAN	SCRIPT	ENGLISH	LATIN	DANISH
Pflasterer		paver	caduceator, filicarius	brulegger
Peitschenmacher		whip maker	- - -	piskemager
Pflugschmied		plowsmith	aratrum faber	plovsmed
Pfluger		plowman	arator	
Pförtner		porter, doorkeeper	porter, calustrarius	portner, portier
Einlasser				
Posamentierer		haberdasher, lace-maker	- - -	småtingshandler
Pottaschbrenner		potash burner	---	pottaske bekker
Posenschaber		quill maker	---	
Kielfederschneider				
Prediger		preacher	---	predikant
Priester		priest	sacerdos	praest
Puppenmaler		painter of religious pictures	- - -	- - -
Puppenmacher		dollmaker	pupa fabricant	dukkemager
Putzfrau		cleaning woman	- - -	rengøring kvinde
Putzhändlerin		milliner	- - -	modelhandler
Putzmacherin		trimming maker	- - -	- -
Quartiermeister		quartermaster	castrorum	kvartermester (coxswain)
Rademacher		wheelwright	- - -	- -
Stellmacher				
Ratsherr		councilman	aksisejer	radmand ?
Ratsmitglied		councilman		
Ratsverwandter		town council assistant	urbs concilium adjutor	grevskapsråd medrjelper
Rechenmeister		accountant, mathematician	abacistus	beretning ---?
Rechtsanwalt		attorney general	cognitor	sagfører, jurist
Reepschläger		rope maker	funis fabricant	rebslager
Reisender		traveler	---	reisende reiser
Reiter		rider, horseman	equitatio, eques	rytter
Reiterei		cavalry	equitatus	kavaleri
Rekrut		recruit	conscribere	rekrutt
Renter		retired person	----	pensioneret
Richter		judge	iudex, quaesitor judix praetor	dommer
Riemenschneider		harness maker	corrigiarius. frenarius, lorarius, lorifex	salsmaker
		leatherworker	corium	laeder (leather dresser)

GERMAN	SCRIPT	ENGLISH	LATIN	DANISH
Ritter		Knight	militis, miles, equester	ridder
Rittmeister		Captain (of calvary)	praefectus	Kaptein
Roggenbrotbäcker		Rye bread baker	- - -	- - -
Rotgerber		tanner	perficere (hides)	garver
Rozenkrantzmacher Päterleinmaker		rosary maker	- - -	rosenkransmager
Sackmacher Säckler		sack maker	crumenarius, bursarius	sekkmaker
Sager		sawyer	---	sager, skjaere
Sänger		singer	cantator	sanger
Salpetersieder		saltpeter-boiler	----	saltpeter koker
Salzhändler		salt trader	salifex, salinator	salt handel- mann
Salzsteuerein- nehmer		salt tax collector	sal tributum	salt skatt samler
Sattler		saddlemaker, leatherworker	stratarius, sellarius. ephipparius	salmaker, sadelmager
Schäfer		sheepherder	oris pastor opilio, bergarius	vok`ter, vogter
Schaffer		steward (Nav.)	dispensator, majordomus	
Schafhirt		sheepherder	pastor	?
Scharfrichter		executioner	carnifex	skarpretter bøddel
Schatzmeister		treasurer	aerari, praefectus	skatt mester
Schieferdecker Leiendecker		slate roofer	- - -	- - -
Schiffbauer		shipbuilder	naupegas	skipsbygger baadebygger
Schiffzimmer- mann		ship's carpenter	---	skibotømrer
Schiffer		sailor (inland waters)	marinarius, nauta	sjomann

GERMAN	SCRIPT	ENGLISH	LATIN	DANISH
Schindelmacher		shingle maker	kaviller	takspĥmaker
Schirmmacher		umbrella maker	umbella fabrikant	paraplymager
Schlachter Metzler		butcher	macellarius	slagter
Schleifer		grinder	samiator, acuciator.eruginator, cotiarius.acuminator, lapsator	grøype maler
Schlosser		locksmith	serator	kleinsmed
Schmelzer		founder, caster molder	flator	synke, støper kaster
Schmied		blacksmith	clusor, faber	grov/med
Schneider Näher, Schrader Schröder		tailor	incisor, sartor nater	skredder skraede´rer
Schneidermeister		master tailor	vestiarius	skraedenmester
Schnürriemenmacher		press workder	- - -	- - -
Schöffe		juror	scabinus	
Schreiber		writer, scribe, clerk	scriptor	forfatter
Schreiner		cabinet maker, joiner carpenter	abiectarius, lignarius	snedker tømmer/mann
Schriftsetzer		typesetter	---	setter, sette-maskin
Schriftsteller, Schreiber		author, writer scribe,copyist	scriba, actuarius	forfatter (m) forfatter-inne (f)
Schüler		student(below university level only	discipulus	studerende
Schuhmacher		shoemaker	coreator, coriarius	skomaker
Schulmeister		schoolmaster	grammaticus, praeceptor	overlærer skolelærer
Schultheiß		village mayor	vicus praefectus scultetus	borgmester
Schuster Flickschuster		shoemaker, cobbler	calcarius lapper	skomaker
Schutzverwandter		stranger, enjoy-ing citizen rights	---	---
Einkömmling Mitterbürger		class between Patrician and a handworker	- - -	- - - -

GERMAN	SCRIPT	ENGLISH	LATIN	DANISH
Schweinehirt		swineherder	sus pastor,	svinehyrde
Seidenwirker		silk weaver	procarius,	
Seidensticker		silk embroiderer	subulcus	silke broderer
Seidenneger			barbaricus	
Seidenkrämer		silk merchant	- - -	- - -
Seemann		seaman	nauta	matros
			navitae	spemand
				sjømann
Seeleute		sailors	navitae	sjømand, matros
Segeltuchmacher		canvass sail maker	- - -	sejlemager ?
Kanefaßmacher				
Seifensieder		soap boiler, soap maker		sæpekoker
Seiler		rope maker	restiarius, cordarius	reipslager
			funarius, restio	
Sensenschmied		scythesmith	faberfalx	sigdsmed,
Sichelschmied		sickelsmith	faberfalx	sigdsmed, krumknivsmed (curved knife)
Siebmacher		sieve maker	cribrarius	silmaker
Siebner		member of committee of 7 to oversee boundaries	- - -	dørslag - - -
Siedler		settler	colonus	kolonist, nybygger
Siegelschneider		engraver	- - -	graverer
Silberschmied		silversmith	aurifaber	sølvsmed
Söldner		mercenary	miles mercen- arius	leid, salgbar
Soldat		soldier	miles	soldat
Spangenmacher		brassworker	orichalcum faber	messingarbeider
Spediteur		dispatcher, merchant	- - -	- - -
Lützenbruder				
Spiegelmacher		mirror maker	catopticus	spei'lmaker
Spielmann		minstrel	fidicen,	skald
Spillemacher		spindle maker	abenteurer,	
Spinnermann		spinner	chelista	
Spitalpfleger		manager or trustee of hospital	- - -	- - -
Sporenschmied		spursmith	artifex- calcarium calcariator	sporesmed
Sporenmacher				
Stadtbote		beadle (minor city official)	urbs minister	stad officiel by officiel
Stadtschreiber		city clerk	urbs scriba	stad skriver
Stallknecht		stable servant groom	stabularis agaso,	stall tjener

GERMAN	SCRIPT	ENGLISH	LATIN	DANISH
Steinbrecher		quarry-man	lapidarius	stein knuse
Steinhauer		stone cutter	lapidare contusip	
Steinklopfer		stone breaker	- - -	- - -
Steinmetz		stone cutter	lapicida	
Stellmacher Rademacher		wheelwright	- - -	- - -
Steuereinnehmer Steuereintreiber		tax collector	collector, exactor	skattsamler
Strumpfweber		stocking weaver	tibiale texérer	strømpe vever strømbevever
Student, Studierender		student(male) university level	---	studerende
Tabaksteuereinnehmer		tobacco tax collector		tobakk skattsamler
Taglöhner Tagelöhner Mietling Hebehauer		day laborer (hireling)	conducticius, laborator mercenarius incola opifex	løsarbeider dagarbeider daglejer
Tierarzt		veterinarian	veterinarius	drylaege(vet.surgeor
Teppichknupfer Heidenwerker		rug weaver tapestry weaver	- - -	taeppevever
Tischler		cabinet maker, furniture maker	mensator, arcularius, arcarius faber	møbelsnekker
Topfer Ofensetzer Ofengießer		potter tile stove maker	figulus,euler, eulner	pottemager
Totengräber		gravedigger	vespillo, fosser fossarius,	---
Topfgießer		steel pot maker	ollarius	- - -
Treideler		one who tows in canal or river	struppa (tow)	buksering
Torwächter		gatekeeper	port(an)arius	- - -
Trommler		drummer	tympanista	trommer
Trödler Höker		second hand dealer	penesticus	brugsthandler
Trompeter		trumpter	trumetter, salpista,	trompeter
Troßknecht		soldier in charge of baggage camp follower	---	---
Truchseß		lord high steward	dominus altes procurator vilicus(estate)	herre høyforvalter

GERMAN	SCRIPT	ENGLISH	LATIN	DANISH
Tuchhändler		textile trader, draper	textilis mercator	teksti´l handler
Tuchmacher		fabric maker	lanifex	kle`deshandler
Kölschenweber Tuchscherer		cloth cutter	- - -	kle`detil´sk
Tüncher Anstreicher Weissbinder		House painter		jaerer
Türhuter		usher	--	dørrokter
Uhrmacher Orleymacher		watchmaker clockmaker	horologiarius	urmaker
Untertan		subject (of a ruler)	homo subditus civis	underkaste
Unvermögender		pauper, penniless	pauper	fattig, tigger
Verkäufer		salesman, merchant	venditor	sel`ger
Vermieter		renter, lessor	------	------
Verwalter Verwaltungsbeamte		administrator	administrator procurator curator	bestyrer
Verweser Pfleger		administrator regent	mamburnus interrex	bestyrer
Veteran		veteran	veteranus	erfaren
Viehhändler Geiseler		cattle trader	pecus mercator	kve´g handler kvaeg handler
Viehhirte		cattle herder	pecus pastor	kve´g hyrde
Vizeburgermeister		vice-mayor	---	vise` borger
Vikar		vicar	vicarius	sogneprest
Vogt, Voigt Sachwalter Verteidiger		warden- senator steward,overseer	advocatus	vokter
Vormund		legal guardian	custos,praeses defensor	formynder
Vorkosthändler Greisler		coarse grain dealer	- - -	- - -
Vorsteher Leiter		chairman, director leader,guide	aedilis, ephorus	

GERMAN	SCRIPT	ENGLISH	LATIN	DANISH
Wachtmeister		sergeant major	optiotribunus militum	sersjant kommander
Wächter		watchman	vigilarius, guardianus, speculator	vak´ter vak´tmann
Waffenschmied		gunsmith, weapon smith	sclopetum faber	børsmaker
Wagner Wagonmacher		wagon builder wagonmaker	carpentarius, rhedarius	wognmaker wognmager karetmager (coachmaker)
Waise		orphan	orbus	foraeldreløs
Waisenpfleger		one who takes care of orphans	- - -	foreld/raus Sykepleierske Sygeplejerske
Waldhüter		forest ranger	Nemorarius	skogmann
Wassermüller		water mill operator	- - -	vand kvaern virker
Wasservogt		water overseer	pristabel	vand tilsybsførende
Weber		weaver	textor	vever, vaever
Wechsler		money changer, banker	commutator, argentarius, cambiator, campsor	bankmand
Wegmacher		path maker, paver	caduceator	sti gangsti brulegger
Wehmutter		midwife	obstetrix	jordsmor
Weinbauer		grape-grower	vinumagricola	vinbonde
Weinhändler		wine trader, vintner	vinum mercator	vin handler
Weinschenker		waiter		
Weißgerber		tanner	albicerdo alutarius cerdo	?
Weißbäker		baker of white bread	similarius	weiss bager
Weißbinder Anstreicher Tüncher		cooper, white-washer	glutinater	bødker
Wirt Schankwirt Gastwirt		innkeeper	caupo, taverner	vertin´ne (f) wert (m)
Wirtschafts- prufer		accountant	calculator	vegnskapsfører
Wollweber		wool weaver	roscher	ullvever
Würfelmacher Wurfeler		dice maker	- - -	terning mager
Wundarzt		surgeon	chirurgus	kirurg
Wurstmacher		sausagemaker	fartor, matiarius	pøl`semaker

GERMAN	SCRIPT	ENGLISH	LATIN	DANISH
Zahnarzt		dentist	dentium medicus	tann´/kge
Zahnbrecher			edentarius	
Zahlmeister		paymaster	- - -	betale mestre
Zeidler		beekeeper	apiarus	biebesitter
Zentgraf		captain	centurio	kaptein dampskibsfører (steamship captian)
Zeuge		witness	testis	vitne
Zeugkrämer		cloth merchant	- -	- -
Ziegelbrenner		brickmaker, owner of a kiln	tegularius, laterator	teglbekker
Zeichner		draftsman, designer	adrumbator	skirserer ?
Ziegeldecker		tiler, roofer, slater	tegulus, imbrex	tegler skifertekker
Ziegler		brickmaker	later fabricant	teglbrender
Zigeuner		gipsy	---	tater, sigøyner
Zimmermann		carpenter	xylocopus carpentarius, lignarius	tømrer snekker snedker
Dübler				
Zinkenist		bugler	buccina	signalhorner
Zinngießer		tinfounder	stannum conditor	tinn, blikk
Kürbenzeiner		pewterer	plumbarius	blikkenslager
Zirkelschmied		compass smith	ambitus farber	kompassmed
Zitzweber		calico weaver	- -	- -
Kattunweber				
Zöllner		toll collecter	telori(e)arius	afgift samler
Zolleinnehmer		customs collector	publicanus	
Zuckerbäcker		confectioner	dulciarius	konditor
Zuchmeister		task master	poenator	arbejdemester
Folterknecht				
Zunftmeister		master of a guild	----	gilde mester
Gewerkmeister				
Kerzenmeister				
Zwirnmacher		thread or twine maker	- -	- -

59

WHAT WAS GOING ON IN THE WORLD AND COMMUNITY OF YOUR ANCESTOR WHEN?

In your research for your ancestors have you ever wondered what their world was like? Have you ever wondered what was going on in the world around them? What were their living conditions? What kind of music were they listening to and what were they reading? Could they read and write?

Genealogy and Family History is more than just names, dates and places. We should realize that they were all people like we are. They had their joys and their disappointments, their good days and bad times, their festival celebrations and their times of mourning. They left their footprints on the sands of time just as each one of us are doing.

On the following pages I have tried to compile some interesting statistics about history, culture, and daily life. I have left a space to the right of the page for you to write in the names of your ancestors. I hope this will give you a small picture of what was going on when your ancestors were living.

I have gathered this information from many, many sources. Please be aware that not all historians and statisticians agree on dates. I could not possibly list all of the wars that went on over the years. How many armies crossed over the land of your ancestors? There may be some differences in dates, but it will give you an idea of what events were affecting the lives of your ancestors.

I want to thank my daughter, Tamara Bentz for helping me compile this information.

Edna Bentz

RELIGIOUS & POLITICAL HISTORY	MUSIC ART & LITERATURE	DAILY LIFE	ANCESTORS
1300 The Renaissance began in Europe 1326 Ottoman Turks invaded Eastern Europe 1337 - 100 years War	1321 Death of Dante following completion of "Divine Comedy"	1300 Temporary end of European slave trade 1327 The Great Fire of Munich, Bavaria 1328 Invention of the saw mill 1332 Bubonic plague originates in India 1334 Black Death begins in Constantinople 1347-1352 Black Death struck Europe. Killed 3/4 population of Europe and Asia 1349 Black Death outbreak in Germany. Blamed on Jews who were cruelly massacred 1354 Mechanical clock installed at Strasbourg Cathedral	

RELIGIOUS & POLITICAL HISTORY	MUSIC, ART & LITERATURE	DAILY LIFE	ANCESTORS
		1361 Black Death reappears in England	
		1366 Fuggers come as weavers to Augsburg	
1370 Hanseatic League Mercantile Assoc. signed treaty with Denmark		1370 Steel crossbow used as weapon of war	
1378 Great Western Schism: Rome & France fight for control of Papacy that lasted until 1417		1377 Playing cards displace dice in Germany	
1379 Peasant revolt in England after Parliment imposed poll tax	1382 John Wycliffe directed translation of the Vulgate Bible into English	1382 Bubonic Plague in Ireland killed thousands. Lasted until 1385	
	1386 Heidelberg University founded by Rupert I Elector of Palatinate		
	1387 Chaucer began to compose "Canterbury Tales"		
1389 Turks defeated Serbs. Serbia became vassal state of Turks		1407 Bubonic Plague in London	
	1409 Leipzig University founded by German emigree from Prague		
1415 John Huss burned at the stake as heretic			
	1427 Thomas à Kempis, German Monk wrote "Imitation of Christ"		
1429 Joan of Arc liberated Orleans			
1431 Joan of Arc burned at the stake			
	1434 Jan van Eyck painted "Arnolfini and Bride"		
1441 Portugese Navigators find negroes in western Africa & start slave trade again		1443 English plague-order on quarantine and cleansing	

RELIGIOUS & POLITICAL HISTORY	MUSIC ART & LITERATURE	DAILY LIFE	ANCESTORS
1448 King Christian I, Denmark-inherits Slesvig-Holstein	1450 Gutenberg begins to print		
1453 End of 100 years War. Constantinople lost to Turks	1454 Gutenberg produces Indulgences bearing printed data		
1455 Wars of the Roses			
	1456 Printing of Mazarin Bible by Gutenberg in Mainz, Germany	1456 Earthquake in Naples 30,000-40,000 killed	
1466 Teutonic Knights ceded Pomerania and West Prussia to Poland	1468 Gutenberg died		
1477 Marriage of Maximillian bringing Low countries to the Hapsburgs	1473 The Sistine Chapel in Vatican was built	1473 Nicholas Copernicus born	
1478 Ferdinand and Isabella instituted the Spanish Inquisition		1479 Brussels becomes center of European Tapestry Industry	
		1480 Rifle invented	
	1481 Botticelli began his Biblical frescoes in Sistine Chapel		
1485 Henry VII of England founded House of Tudor		1488 First apotheke in Berlin	
		1490 First orphanages in Italy & Holland	
		1491 Fire in Dresden	
1492 Christopher Columbus voyages to America		1492 Profession of book publishers emerges	
1493 Inca Empire begins	1494 Leonardo DaVinci painted "The Last Supper"	1494 Columbus brings corn back to Spain. Cultivated at first for cattle-food. Then to the table of poor	
1497 John Cabot explored northeast coast to Delaware Portugal expelled Jews who refused Catholic conversion		1498 First German Pawnshop in Nüremberg	

RELIGIOUS & POLITICAL HISTORY	MUSIC ART & LITERATURE	DAILY LIFE	ANCESTORS
		1499 Bubonic Plague in London	
		1500 Corn became major food in form of por-ridge. Deficiency disease developed similar to beriberi later named pellagra Watch invented First black lead pencils in England First recorded Caesarean operation performed on a living woman by a Swiss pig gelder	
1501 Amerigo Vespucci explored coast of Brazil	1501 Michaelangelo sculpts "David"	1501 Card games gain popularity all over Europe	
	1503 Leonardo DaVinci paints "Mona Lisa"	1503 Pocket handkerchief comes into use	
	1506 Basilica of St. Peter's in Rome started		
1508 Maximillian be-comes "Emperor Elect" and "King of Germany"	1508 Michelangelo works on "Sistine Chapel"		
1513 Ponce deLeon dis-covers Florida Balboa discovers Pacific	1513 Michelangelo sculpts "Moses" Raphael painted "Sistine Madona" Macchiavelli wrote "The Prince"	1514 Pineapples arrive in Europe	
1517 Martin Luther nails thesis to Wittenberg Church door		1517 Coffee in Europe for first time	
1518 Luther's appear-ance at Augs-burg Diet			
1519 Cortez defeats Aztecs Maximillian I died Magellan goes around the world Zwingli began Reformation in Switzerland			

RELIGIOUS & POLITICAL HISTORY	MUSIC MUSIC & LITERATURE	DAILY LIFE	ANCESTORS
1520 Luther excommunicated			
1520 Luther translates New Testament into German		1522 Imperial Diet of Nürnberg studied problems of Monopolies because of their grave effects upon general living standards	
1524 Peasants Revolt in Black Forest spreads to other parts of Germany	1524 Luther prints his first "Gesangbuch"		
	1530 Augsburg Confession adopted	1528 Typhus Epidemic in Italy	
		1530 Potato first discovered by Spaniards in Peru	
1532 Nürnberg Peace Treaty		1531 Earthquake in Lisbon, Portugal	
1533 Ivan IV (the terrible) begins reign in Russia			
1534 Henry VIII founds the Anglican Church Luther completes translation of Bible into German St. Ignatius Loyola founded Jesuit order	1534 Michelangelo paints "The Last Judgement"		
1535 Sir Thomas More beheaded			
1536 Anne Boleyn executed Henry VIII marries Jane Seymour Reformation in Norway and Denmark			
1539 DeSoto discovers the Mississippi		1539 First Christmas Tree at Strasbourg Cathedral	
	1540 Hans Holbein the Younger paints "Henry VIII"		

RELIGIOUS & POLITICAL HISTORY	MUSIC ART & LITERATURE	DAILY LIFE	ANCESTORS
1545 Council of Trent		1543 Nicholas Copernicus published his astronomy discoveries	
1546 Martin Luther died			
1548 Diet of Augsburg		1550 Potato appears in Spain	
1555 Peace of Augsburg		1557 Influenza epidemic all over Europe	
	1559 Pope Paul IV established the Index of Forbidden Books		
1560 Lutheran becomes State religion in Denmark	1561 Francis Bacon born		
1563 Counter Reformation begins in Bavaria		1563 Plague in Europe kills 20,000 in London	
1565 St. Augustine, Fla. founded	1565 Pieter Bruegel the Elder paints "Peasant Wedding"		
	1568 Pieter Bruegel the Elder paints "The Peasant Dance"	1570 Nürnberg postal service begun	
1576 Martin Frobisher searched for Northwest Passage. Maximillian II died Rudolf II succeeds			
1577 Lutheran Book of Concord drafted			
	1582 Douay version of New Testament published	1582 Gregorian calendar introduced	
		1584 Potato brought to England from North America	
		1589 Forks first used in France	
		1595 First heels on shoes	
		1596 Galileo invents thermometer	

RELIGIOUS & POLITICAL HISTORY	MUSIC, ART & LITERATURE	DAILY LIFE		ANCESTORS
		1599 First German postal rates fixed		
	1600 Shakespeare writes "Hamlet"			
		1601 German brothels closed because of venereal disease		
	1602 Shakespeare writes "Alls Well that Ends Well"	1602 Galileo discovers gravity		
1603 James VI of Scotland became James I of England founding House of Stuart	1606 Rembrandt born	1603 Bubonic Plague in London		
1607 Jamestown founded				
1608 Champlain founded Quebec		1608 Galileo constructs telescope		
	1609 Douay version of Old Testament published	1609 Bank of Amsterdam founded Newspaper started in Germany		
1610 Formation of Catholic League	1610 Shakespeare writes "A Winter's Tale" Michelangelo died	1610 Galileo sees Jupiter's satellites		
1611 King James version of Bible published	1616 Shakespeare died			
1617 John Calvin's works published				
1618 Thirty Years War begun		1618 Diphtheria epidemic in Naples		
1619 First Negro slaves in No. America arrive in Virginia		1619 William Harvey discovered circulation of blood		
1620 Pilgrims arrived at Plymouth, Mass. on Mayflower		1620 Currency inflation in Germany		
		1621 First potatoes planted in Germany		
		1622 January 1st declared beginning of year in Germany. Used to be March 25th.		

RELIGIOUS & POLITICAL HISTORY	MUSIC, ART & LITERATURE	DAILY LIFE	ANCESTORS
		1624 Fire destroys Oslo, Norway	
		1625 Bubonic Plague in London	
1626 Manhattan purchased from Indians			
		1628 Typhus Epidemic in Lyons, France	
1630 Massachuetts Bay Colony formed			
1631 Earthquake at Naples, Italy Eruption of Vesuvius			
		1632 Galileo published his work confirming Copernican theory of astronomy	
		1633 Outbreak of Plague in Bavaria leads to Passion Play Vow	
	1634 Passion Play for first time in Oberammergau		
1640 Puritan Revolution in England began			
		1642 Galileo died	
		1643 Barometer invented by Evanelista Torricelli	
1648 Peace of Westphalia - End 30 Years War		1648 Population of Germany dropped from 17 million to 8 million due to 30 Years War and the plague	
1649 King Charles I beheaded			
		1650 World Population 510 million	
		1659 Typhoid fever described by Thomas Willis	
		1665 Great Plague of London	
		1666 Fire destroys 14,000 Buildings in London	
1669 Mt. Etna Erupted in Italy	1669 Rembrandt died	1670 Diabetes described by Thomas Willis	
		1671 Leibniz discovers ether	
		1672 Bubonic Plague in Lyons, France Bubonic Plague in Naples	

RELIGIOUS & POLITICAL HISTORY	MUSIC, ART & LITERATURE	DAILY LIFE	ANCESTOR
	1675 Cathedral of St. Paul's, London started		
1682 Peter the Great begins reign in Russia. Established schools and newspapers	1685 Johann Sebastian Bach born Georg Friederich Händel born	1685 Newton published his theories of motion & gravitation 1688 Plate glass cast for first time	
1689 German diet declares war on France Heidelberg Castle destroyed		1694 Fire destroys 1/2 of Warwick, England	
1697 Last remains of Mayas destroyed		1700 World population 625 million The commode becomes popular	
1701 Hohenzollerns come to power Frederick becomes King of Prussia		1701 Invention of sowing drill	
1702 Asiento Guinea Co. founded slave trade between Africa & America		1702 Many German towns now lit by oil 1703 Great Storm in England killed 8,000	
1706 Benjamin Franklin born			
1707 Perpetual Alliance signed between Prussia and Sweden Great Britain formed by England & Scotland		1707 Eruption of Mt.Fujiyama in Japan 1708/9 Exceeding cold winter killed all of the crops. Farm prices low, Taxes high.	
1709 Great emigration from German speaking area to America		1711 Bubonic Plague in Germany and Austria	
1713 Frederick Wilhelm I comes to power in Prussia as King		1712 Newcomen invents steam pump which aided coal mining	
1714 Georg I began rule of England		1714 D. G. Fahrenheit constructs mercury thermometer Witch trials abolished in Prussia	
1715 Age of Enlightenment began			

RELIGIOUS & POLITICAL HISTORY	MUSIC, ART & LITERATURE	DAILY LIFE	ANCESTOR
		1717 Inoculation for smallpox introduced in England. Few received it. School attendance in Prussia made compulsory.	
		1720 Bubonic Plague in Marseilles, France	
		1727 Isaac Newton died	
		1728 Fire nearly destroys Copenhagen	
	1731 Benjamin Franklin founds library system		
	1732 Benjamin Franklin prints "Poor Richard's Almanac" Josephus Haydn born	1732 Threshing machine by Michael Menzies	
		1733 Paul Revere born	
1738 John Wesley began preaching in England		1738 First cuckoo clocks made in Black Forest	
1740 Maria Theresa rules Hapsburg Empire First Silesian War War of Austrian Succession: a general European War. Ended 1748		1740 Smallpox epidemic in Berlin Frederick the Great introduces freedom of the press and freedom of worship in Prussia	
	1741 Handel writes "The Messiah"		
1744 Second Silesian War			
1745 Peace at Dresden			
		1749 Sign language for deaf invented	
1750 Industrial Revolution begun	1750 Johann Sebastian Bach died	1750 World population 710 million	
	1751 First Encyclopedia edited by Diderot and d'Alembert		
		1752 Benjamin Franklin invents lightening rod Fire destroys 18,000 homes in Moscow, Russia	

RELIGIOUS & POLITICAL HISTORY	MUSIC ART & LITERATURE	DAILY LIFE	ANCESTOR
1754 French and Indian Wars started in North America			
		1755 Lisbon earthquake kills 30,000	
1756 Seven Years War	1756 Wolfgang Amadeus Mozart born	1756 First chocolate factory in Germany	
1758 East Prussia occupied by Russia	1759 Handel died		
1760 Georg II began 60-yr. reign in England		1761 Venus first observed	
1762 Catherine II (the great) begins reign in Russia		1762 Catherine II of Russia promoted education, the arts & social reforms	
1763 End of Seven Years War		1763 Frederick the Great establishes village schools in Prussia	
		1764 Numbering system for houses begun in England Mechanization of textile spinning	
1765 American Stamp Act		1765 Potato becomes most popular food in Europe Watt perfects steam engine	
1766 Repeal of Stamp Act Mason-Dixon Line drawn			
		1767 Town planning on a grand scale began in Edinburgh, Scotland	
1770 Boston Massacre	1770 Ludwig von Beethovan born		
1773 Holstein ceded to Denmark		1772 Poland partitioned among Russia, Austria & Prussia	
1774 Louis XVI & Marie Antoinette become King & Queen of France			
1775 Paul Revere's Ride American Revolution began			
1776 Signing of Declaration of Independence			

RELIGIOUS & POLITICAL HISTORY	MUSIC, ART & LITERATURE	DAILY LIFE	ANCESTOR
1778 War of Bavarian Succession Act of Congress prohibits import of slaves			
		1780 Bifocal lens made by Benjamin Franklin First fountain pen constructed	
		1781 Uranus first viewed	
		1784 First iron plow by James Small First school for the blind in Paris	
		1786 Earliest attempts at internal gas lighting in Germany	
1787 U. S. Constitution signed			
1788 British Parliament motion for abolition of slave trade		1788 Dollar currency introduced in USA	
1789 George Washington becomes first President of USA French Revolution			
1790 U. S. Capital moved to Philadelphia Benjamin Franklin died			
1791 Bill of Rights ratified USA	1791 Thomas Paine wrote "The Rights of Man" directed against critics of French Revolution		
1792 Denmark first nation to abolish slave trade		1793 Eli Whitney invents cotton gin. Yellow Fever epidemic in Philadelphia	
1793 U. S. law compels escaped slaves to return to their owners	1794 Thomas Paine wrote "The Age of Reason"	1794 Francois Appert designs preserving jar for foods	
1794 Slavery abolished in French colonies.		1796 Edward Jenner introduced smallpox vaccine made from cow-pox virus in England	

RELIGIOUS & POLITICAL HISTORY	MUSIC, ART & LITERATURE	DAILY LIFE	ANCESTOR
1797 John Adams becomes President of USA	1797 Franz Schubert born		
1799 Georg Washington died Napoleon Bonaparte overthrew existing French government		1799 Napoleon Bonaparte reformed legal system	
1800 Washington, D.C. made Capital of USA		1800 Socialism developed in Europe in reaction to deplorable industrial conditions World population 910 million	
1801 Thomas Jefferson becomes President of USA		1801 Steam locomotive perfected by Richard Trevithick	
		1802 John Dalton introduced atomic theory into chemistry First factory law introduced in England pertaining to child labor	
1803 Louisiana Purchase	1803 Ralph Waldo Emerson born		
1804 Hamilton-Burr duel Napoleon assumes the Imperial title	1804 Johann Strauss, Sr. born Folk melodies became favorable		
1806 Prussia declares war on France Official end of Holy Roman Empire	1806 Elizabeth Barrett Browning born	1806 Population of Germany 27 million	
1807 England prohibits slave trade	1807 Henry Wadsworth Longfellow born	1807 Robert Fulton navigates paddle steamer on Hudson River	
1808 U.S. prohibits import of slaves from Africa	1808 Goethe wrote "Faust"	1808 Municipal Councils introduced in Prussia	

RELIGIOUS & POLITICAL HISTORY	MUSIC, ART & LITERATURE	DAILY LIFE	ANCESTOR
1809 Peace of Schön-brunn James Madison becomes President of USA	1809 Edgar Allan Poe born Charles Darwin born Thomas Paine died Joseph Haydn died Felix Mendelssohn born Abraham Lincoln born	1809 Louis Braille invents reading system for the blind	
1810 Mexico begins fight to gain independence from Spain	1810 Frederic Francois Chopin born 1811 Franz Liszt born	1810 U. S. Population 7,239,881 Mowing machine invented by Peter Gaillard	
1812 U.S. declares war on Britian	1812 Charles Dickens born Robert Browning born Grimm's Fairy-tales written 1813 Richard Wagner born Waltz conquers Europe	1812 Revival of German mythology and folk tales Jews in Prussia emancipated	
1815 Napoleon exiled		1815 Miners safety lamp invented by Humphry Davy Income tax ended in England John Macadam constructs first road of crushed stone	
1816 English economic crisis causes large scale emigration to U.S.A. & Canada	1816 Charlotte Bronte born American Bible Society founded	1816 Stethoscope invented by R. T. Laenner Typhoid Epidemic in Ireland. 1/4 population dies. Ended in 1819	
1817 Lutheran & Re-formed Churches in Prussia form Evangelical Union James Monroe becomes President of USA	1817 Henry David Thoreau born		

RELIGIOUS & POLITICAL HISTORY	MUSIC, ART & LITERATURE	DAILY LIFE	ANCESTOR
	1818 Franz Xaver Gruber and Austrian School teacher wrote music to Joseph Mohr's words "Stille Nacht, Heilige Nacht"		
1819 Freedom of the Press in France		1819 Maximum 12 hour working day for juveniles in England	
		1820 Cultivator made by Henry Burden	
1821 Mexico gains independence	1822 Louis Pasteur born		
1823 Monroe Doctrine		1823 Charles Macintosh invents waterproof fabric First Cologne Carnival festivities Death penalty for over 100 crimes abolished in Britain	
1824 Erie Canal finished		1824 Beginning of German emigration to Brazil	
1825 John Quincy Adams becomes President of USA	1825 Johann Straus (the son) born	1825 Horse drawn buses in London Tractor by Robert Keeley	
	1827 Beethoven died	1827 Joseph Niepce produces photographs on metal plate Sulfur friction matches introduced by John Walker James Simpson constructs sand filter for purification of London's water supply	
1829 Andrew Jackson becomes President of USA Catholic Emancipation of Great Britain to sit in Parliament & hold most public offices	1828 Noah Webster's "American Dictionary" of English Language Schubert died		
1830 Mormon church founded by Joseph Smith		1830 Earl von Reichenbach discovers paraffin	

RELIGIOUS & POLITICAL HISTORY	MUSIC, ART & LITERATURE	DAILY LIFE	ANCESTOR
		1830 Ladies skirts grow shorter, sleeves become enormous, hats extremely large ornamented with flowers and ribbons Stiff collars become part of man's dress	
1831 London Bridge opened Russians suppressed Polish insurrection, beginning of "Russification" of Poland	1831 "America" written by Samuel Francis Smith. National anthem until 1931	1831 First horse drawn buses in New York German emigration to America 15,000 Cholera begins in India 1826 spreads from Russia into Central Europe reaching Scotland 1832 Electric generator by Hippolyte Pixii	
1833 Slavery barred in British Empire	1833 Johannes Brahms born	1834 Cyrus Hall McCormick patents reaping machine Disastrous fire in Britain Houses of Parliament	
	1835 Mark Twain (Samuel Langhorne Clemens) born Phineas Taylor Barnum begins his career	1835 First German RR line opens between Nürnberg & Furth Halley's comet reappears Fire in New York City destroys 700 buildings Samuel Colt patents single barreled pistol & rible Smallpox vaccination became mandatory in England and Wales 1098 miles of railroad in use in USA	
1837 Reign of Queen Victoria England enjoyed era of prosperity England introduces official birth registrations Financial and economic panic in America Martin Van Buren President of USA	1838 Best Sellers "Oliver Twist" and "Nicholas Nickleby" by Charles Dickins Jenny Lind makes debut in Stockholm, Sweden		

RELIGIOUS & POLITICAL HISTORY	MUSIC, ART & LITERATURE	DAILY LIFE	ANCESTOR
1839 First wagon-train from New York to Oregon ordered by Pres. Andrew Jackson started west		1839 Prussia restricts juvenile labor to a maximum of 10 hours per day Charles Goodyear discovers process of vulcanization making possible commercial use of rubber First electric clock built in Switzerland by Carl August Steinheil First bicycle built by Kirkpatrick Macmillian	
	1840 Pietr Ilich Tchaikovsky born	1840 World-wide Cholera pandemic claimed millions. Ended 1862	
1841 William Henry Harrison President USA 1 month John Tyler President USA		1841 German emigration to America 43,000 First university degrees granted to women in America	
	1842 Polka comes into fashion	1842 Fire in Hamburg destroys much of city Crawford W. Long uses ether to produce surgical anesthesia	
	1843 Dickins "A Christmas Carol" written	1843 Skiing begins as a sport in Norway	
	1844 Poe wrote "The Raven and other Poems"	1844 First public bath & wash houses opened in Liverpool, England Wood-pulp paper invented by Friedrich Gottlob Keller Y.M.C.A. founded by George Williams	
1845 James K. Polk becomes President of USA		1845 Smallpox vaccination manditory in Scotland and Ireland Telegraph invented by Samuel Morse	

RELIGIOUS & POLITICAL HISTORY	MUSIC, ART & LITERATURE	DAILY LIFE	ANCESTORS
1846 Mexico-American War lasted until 1848	1846 First painted Christmas card designed by John C. Horseley	1846 Famine in Ireland caused by failure of potato crop until 1851. One million people died of starvation and disease. Hundreds of thousands left the country Bad harvests in Europe until 1847 Cholera epidemic First sewing machine perfected by Elias Howe	
1847 Mormons find Salt Lake City, Utah USA	1847 Felix Mendelssohn died Charlotte Bronte wrote "Jane Eyre" Emily Bronte wrote "Wuthering Heights"	1847 Evaporated milk made for first time Alexander G. Bell born J. T. Semmelweis, Hungarian physician discovers connection between childbed fever and puerperal infection British restrict working day for women & children to 10 hours Influenza epidemic in London, England killed 15,000	
1848 Gold discovered in California USA Communist Manifesto issued by Marx & Engels Revolution in France, Germany, Austria, Hungary, Bohemia & Italy Reign of Francis Joseph, Emperor of Austria		1848 First appendectomy by Hancock Serfdom abolished in Austria First Public Health Act in Britain	
	1849 Frederic Chopin died Dickens wrote "David Copperfield" "Who's Who" begins publication in USA	1849 Speed of Light measured Fire in St. Louis, Mo. USA destroys 15 blocks	

RELIGIOUS & POLITICAL HISTORY	MUSIC, ART & LITERATURE	DAILY LIFE	ANCESTOR
1850 Church Council to manage Protestant Churches in Prussia Millard Fillmore President of USA	1850 Hawthorne wrote "The Scarlet Letter" Jenny Lind tours America with P. T. Barnum	1850 Gas burner produced by R. W. Bunsen World population 1,130 million First windows that could open	
	1851 Hawthorne wrote "The House of Seven Gables" Herman Melville wrote "Moby Dick"	1851 Sewing machine with continuous stitch invented by Issac Singer First double-decker bus Tuberculosis epidemic in England killed average 51,000 per year. Lasted until 1855	
1852 Reign of Napoleon III Emperor of Second French Empire		1852 U. S. imports sparrows from Germany as defense against caterpillers	
1853 Franklin Pierce President of USA		1853 First railroad thru the Alps (Vienna, Austria - Trieste) Alexander Wood uses hypodermic syringe for subcutaneous injections Queen Victoria allows chloroform to be administered to her during birth of 7th child. Insures its place as anesthetic in Britain	
1854 Crimean War begins until 1856	1854 Thoreau wrote "Walden or Life in the Woods"		
1855 Paris World Fair Reign of Alexander II in Russia	1855 Longfellow writes "The Song of Hiawatha" Russian literature began its most creative period	1855 London sewers modernized after outbreak of Cholera Florence Nightingale introduces hygienic standards into Military hospitals	
		1856 Black Forest railroad with 40 tunnels opened "Big Ben" cast named after Benjamin Hall Bessemer invented process of converting iron into steel	

RELIGIOUS & POLITICAL HISTORY	MUSIC, ART, & LITERATURE	DAILY LIFE	ANCESTORS
1857 James Buchanan President of USA Financial & economic crisis throughout Europe caused by speculation in U.S. rail shares		1857 Pasteur proves fermentation is caused by living organisms Otis installs first safety elevator Matrimonial Causes Act in Britain Transatlantic Cable started	
	1859 Dickens wrote "Tale of two Cities" Darwin wrote "Origin of the Species"	1859 Steamroller invented Suez Canal begun	
1860 English Church Union founded Food & Drug Act enacted in Britain			
1861 Kingdom of Italy proclaimed. Victor Emmanuel IV becomes King Rumania formed by unification of Moldavia & Walachin U. S. introduces passport system Russia emancipates serfs Abraham Lincoln President of USA Civil War in USA to 1865	1861 Dickens wrote "Great Expectations"	1861 Chilled cold-storage unit built by T. S. Mart Pasteur presents "germ theory" Daily weather forcast began in Britain	
1862 Otto von Bismarck became premier and chancellor of Prussia		1862 10-Barrel gun constructed by R. J. Gattling	
		1863 London Underground Railroad Scarlet Fever Epidemic in London, Eng. kills more than 30,000 Worldwide Cholera pandemic	
1864 Prussian war with Denmark. Denmark loses Slesvig-Holstein and area up to Ribe		1864 Louis Pasteur invents pasteurization for wine	

RELIGIOUS & POLTICAL HISTORY	MUSIC, ART & LITERATURE	DAILY LIFE	ANCESTORS
1865 Slavery abolished in USA William Booth organizes Salvation Army Andrew Johnson President of USA	1865 Lewis Carroll wrote "Adventures of Alice in Wonderland" Mark Twain "The Celebrated Jumping Frog of Calaveras County"	1865 Thaddeus Lowe invents ice machine Carpet sweeper comes into use Ku Klux Klan founded Railroad sleeping car designed by George M. Pullman First train holdup in North Bend, Ohio	
1866 Austria-Prussian War "Black Friday" on London Stock Exchange		1866 Prussia lost 120,000 in Cholera epidemic Austria lost 110,000 in Cholera epidemic Portland Maine destroyed by fire Fire in Quebec destroys 2500 buildings Alfred Nobel invents dynamite Robert Whitehead invents underwater torpedo Permanent Trans-Continental Cable laid Livingstone explores the Congo	
1867 Prussia controlled north Germany Canadian Provinces United Russia sold Alaska to USA	1867 Marx published first volume "Das Kapital" Johann Strauss (the son) composes "Blue Danube" Waltz		
1868 Benjamin Disraeli and William Gladstone vie for control of prime ministry of England Austrian schools freed from Church control	1868 Louisa M. Alcott wrote "Little Women"	1868 Oleomargarine first made by Hippolyte Mege-Mourtiz	
1869 Ulysses S.Grant President of USA		1869 British debtors' prisons are abolished First post cards introduced in Austria Air-brake invented by George Westinghouse	

RELIGIOUS & POLITICAL HISTORY	MUSIC, ART & LITERATURE	DAILY LIFE	ANCESTORS
1870 Standard Oil. founded by John D. Rockefeller Prussian war with France loss of Alsace-Lorraine Dogma of Papal Infallibility declared by Vatican Vladimir Lenin founder of Modern Communism is born		1870 Stock ticker invented by Thomas A. Edison	
1871 German Empire proclaimed William I Emperor of German Empire North & South Germany became united into single Reich	1871 Lewis Carroll wrote "Through the Looking Glass" Louisa May Alcott wrote "Little Men"	1871 Over 1 million acres burned in Michigan & Wisconsin Great Fire in Chicago 3.5 sq. miles destroyed	
1872 Jesuits expelled from Germany	1872 Whistler paints "The Artist's Mother"	1872 Boston Fire 600 dwellings burn Motion Pictures invented by E. Muybridge & John D. Isaacs	
1873 Financial panic in USA lasted 5 yrs.		1873 Color photographs developed E. Remington & Sons begin to produce typewriters Germany adopts the Mark as its unit of currency	
1874 Civil marriage is made compulsory in Germany		1874 Smallpox vaccination mandatory in Germany Billroth discovers streptococci and staphylococci First American zoo established in Philadelphia H. Solomon introduces pressure-cooking methods Barbed wire invented by J. F. Glidden	
1875 Civil Rights Act was passed forbidding discrimination of blacks in public bldgs. Movement for Irish independence started by Charles Stewart Parnell	1875 Mark Twain wrote "The Adventures of Tom Sawyer"		

RELIGIOUS & POLITICAL HISTORY	MUSIC, ART & LITERATURE	DAILY LIFE	ANCESTOR
		1876 Gas engine invented by Nikolaus August Otto Telephone invented by Alexander G.Bell	
1877 Rutherford Hayes President of USA		1877 Phonograph invented by Thomas A.Edison First public phone in USA	
1878 Congress of Berlin. Much of Ottoman Empire divided among Russia, Britain & Austro-Hungarian Empire		1878 Microphone invented by David Hughes Karl Benz builds motorized tricycle Electric street lighting in London First European crematorium established in Gothe,Germany Yellow Fever epidemic southern USA kills 14,000	
1879 Anti-Jesuit Laws introduced in France			
		1880 Cologne Cathedral completed-begun in 1248 Edison devises first practical electric lights Pasteur discovers a Chicken Cholera vaccine Canned fruits & meats first appear in stores Evaporated milk by John Meyenberg	
1881 James A. Garfield President of USA 6 mos. Chester A Arthur President of USA Alexander II of Russia assassinated			
1882 Triple Alliance formed by Germany, Austria-Hungary & Italy	1882 Mark Twain wrote "The Prince and the Pauper"		
1883 Supreme Court rules parts of Civil Rights Act of 1875 invalid opening way for repassage of Jim Crow laws in USA	1883 Wagner died Robert Lewis Stevenson wrote "Treasure Island"	1883 Invention of electric flatiron by H.W. Seely Worldwide Cholera epidemic until 1894 killed millions	

RELIGIOUS & POLITICAL HISTORY	MUSIC, ART & LITERATURE	DAILY LIFE	ANCESTORS
	1884 Mark Twain wrote "Huckelberry Finn"	1884 Linotype invented by Ottomar Mergenthaler	
1885 Grover Cleveland President of USA		1885 Louis Pasteur used vaccine to prevent rabies in young boy Dictating machine invented by Charles S. Tainter	
	1886 Franz Liszt died	1886 American Federation of Labor organized Statue of Liberty unveiled in NY harbor	
		1887 Kiel Canal started between North Sea & Baltic Sea	
	1888 Louisa May Alcott died	1888 Big Blizzard in USA	
1889 Oklahoma "land rush" opened all but panhandle of Okla. Terr. for settlement Benjamin Harrison President of USA		1889 Influenza epidemic worldwide affected 40% of world population until 1891	
1893 Financial panic caused partly by severe gold drain began; thousands of banks and commercial institutions failed before economy recovered in 1897 USA	1893 Tschaikovsky died	1893 Zipper invented by Whitcomb L. Judson	
1894 Dreyfus Affair until 1906 Reign of Nicholas II last tsar of Russia		1894 Fire in Hinkley, Minn. destroys more than 160,000 acres forest	
		1895 Kiel Canal completed Roentgen discovered Xrays Marconi sent message over wireless	
		1896 Electric stove invented by Wm. S. Hadaway, Jr.	
1897 William McKinley President of USA Gold rush in Klondike began	1897 Brahms died		

RELIGIOUS & POLITICAL HISTORY	MUSIC ART & LITERATURE	DAILY LIFE	ANCESTORS
1898 Spanish-American War U.S. annexed Hawaii	1898 Lewis Carroll died	1898 Zeppelin invented, motor driven airship and made first trial flight two years later The Curies discovered radium	
1899 U.S. participates in First Hague Conference which established Permanent Court of Arbitration Cuba became independent republic under US protection	1899 Strauss (the son) died		
		1900 World population 1,600 million	
1901 President Wm. McKinley assassinated Theodore Roosevelt became President of USA			
		1903 Airplane invented by Orville & Wilbur Wright	
		1905 Einstein formulated theory of relativity	
1906 Britain launched the "Dreadnought" first large battleship signaling start of world naval buildup		1906 San Francisco Earthquake 250,000 homeless	
		1908 Hellicopter (man carrying invented by Paul Cornu)	
1910 Reign of Georg V of Great Britain	1910 Mark Twain died		
1911 Italy declared war on Turkey			
1912 Balkan War between Balkan countries & Turkey			
1913 European nations increased preparations for war			
1914 Assassination of Archduke of Austria sparked World War I		1914 Panama Canal opened	
1920 North Schleswig given back to Denmark			

84

PRACTICING THE A, B, C'S

When I was a little girl, my mother taught me the song below. She also taught it to our children. Learning something like this with a song will make it remain in your memory bank. I found this song in an old school song book of my father's. It was printed in 1884 and he sang out of it in the 1890s. You may have learned the English A, B. C's with the same melody.

Sing it first reading the old Gothic print and then when you know the melody, try singing it from the Script.

145. 𝔄 𝔅 ℭ.

𝔄 𝔅 ℭ 𝔇 𝔈 𝔉 𝔊   ℌ 𝔍 𝔍 𝔎 𝔏 𝔐 𝔑 𝔒 𝔓   𝔒 𝔔 𝔖 𝔗 𝔘 𝔙 𝔚

𝔒 𝔔 𝔖 𝔗 𝔘 𝔙 𝔚   𝔛 𝔜p = si = lon 𝔷 — o weh! kann's ja nicht ler = nen, das 𝔄 𝔅 ℭ.

GERMAN SCRIPT		ENGLISH PHONETIC PRONUNCIATION	GERMAN SCRIPT		ENGLISH PHONETIC PRONUNCIATION
		ah			enn
		bay			oh
		tsay			pay
		day			koo
		ay			air
		eff			ess
		gay			tay
		hah			oo
		ee			fow
		yot			vay
		kah			iks
		ell			ipsilon
		emm			tset

hang in there

IF I CAN
YOU CAN!

Mind Glück
Edna

ORDINALS

1	erste(n)	_(handwritten)_
2	zweite(n)	_(handwritten)_
3	dritte(n)	_(handwritten)_
4	vierte(n)	_(handwritten)_
5	fünfte(n)	_(handwritten)_
6	sechste(n)	_(handwritten)_
7	siebte, siebente(n)	_(handwritten)_
8	achte(n)	_(handwritten)_
9	neunte(n)	_(handwritten)_
10	zente(n)	_(handwritten)_
11	elfte(n)	_(handwritten)_
12	zwölfte(n)	_(handwritten)_
13	dreizehnte(n)	_(handwritten)_
14	viersehnte(n)	_(handwritten)_
15	fünfzehnte(n)	_(handwritten)_
16	sechszehnte(n)	_(handwritten)_
17	siebzehnte(n)	_(handwritten)_
18	actzehnte(n)	_(handwritten)_
19	neunzehnte(n)	_(handwritten)_
20	zwanzigste(n)	_(handwritten)_
21	einundzwanzigste(n)	_(handwritten)_
22	zweiundzwanzigste(n)	_(handwritten)_
23	dreiundzwanzigste(n)	_(handwritten)_
24	vierundzwanzigste(n)	_(handwritten)_
25	fünfundzwanzigste(n)	_(handwritten)_
26	sechsundzwanzigste(n)	_(handwritten)_
27	siebenundzwanzigste(n)	_(handwritten)_
28	achtundzwanzigste(n)	_(handwritten)_
29	neunundszwanzigste (n)	_(handwritten)_
30	dreißigste(n)	_(handwritten)_

ORDINALS (Continued)

31   einunddreißigate (n)   *(handwritten: einundreißigaten (n))*

Dates are often found written with ordinal numbers (first, second, third, etc.
or 1st, 2nd, 3rd, etc.) In German ordinal numbers may be written with a period "."
after the number such as 1., 2., 3., or by adding the endings e, te, ten, ste,
stem. depending on the number and the case.

TIME

ein Uhr		one o'clock
zwei, swey Uhr		two o'clock
drei, drey Uhr		three o'clock
vier Uhr		four o'clock
fünf Uhr		five o'clock
sechs Uhr		six o'clock
sieben Uhr		seven o'clock
act Uhr		eight o'clock
neun Uhr		nine o'clock
zehn Uhr		ten o'clock
elf Uhr		eleven o'clock
zwölf Uhr		twelve o'clock

früh - early, a.m.

spät - late, p.m.

abend(s) = evening

mittag(s) = noon

mitternacht(s) = midnight

morgan(s) = morning

nachmittag(s) afternoon

nachmitternacht(s) = after midnight

halb eins = half one (12:30)

halb zwei = (1:30)

etc.

Note: in German, the word halb
preceding the hour means one-half
before the hour, NOT one-half hour
past the hour